The
Connell Guide
to
Shakespeare's

———

Macbeth

———

by
Graham Bradshaw

D1242269

Contents

So what of the play's final scene?
Is it or isn't it triumphal?   101

Is life a tale "told by an idiot/
Signifying nothing"?   108

NOTES

Introduction

Even now, whenever I read *Macbeth*, I cannot forget the terror I felt when I first read it as an eight-year-old boy in Brazil who was certainly no swot, and read anything he could get hold of, including the notorious American horror comics that were banned in Britain and many other countries. The comics were frightening, in their lurid way. But the first act of *Macbeth* seemed like a far more dreadful imaginative summons. I still remember the shock of realizing that blood must reek, or have a smell, and that in Scotland, which must be a very cold country, bloody swords would smoke. I remember my shuddering horror when I guessed, with the help of the word "unseam", just what it was that Macbeth was doing to Macdonwald when he ripped him open from the nave to the chops – and my incredulity when Duncan's response was to call this disemboweller of rebels a "Worthy gentleman"! Was the King of Scotland even listening to the terrifying report from the bleeding Captain?

Macbeth may well be the most terrifying play in the English language, but it hasn't always been seen that way. It has divided critics more deeply than any other Shakespearian tragedy – and the argument, in essence, has been about just how terrifying the play really is and about how we should react, or do react, to Macbeth himself. No Shakespearian tragedy gives as much attention to its hero as *Macbeth*. With the exception of Lady Macbeth, there is much less emphasis on the figures round the hero than there is in *Hamlet* or *Othello*. Unlike *King Lear,* with its parallel story of Gloucester and his sons, *Macbeth* has no sub-plot. There is little comedy, so little that many find the porter's scene, the one exception, a jarring addition to the play. And its imagery of sharp contrasts – of day and night, light and dark, innocent life and murder – adds to the almost claustrophobic intensity of this most intense of plays.

So why are critics so divided about *Macbeth*? Why is it such a disturbing play? Why do we feel compelled to admire its hero even as we condemn him? How reassuring is the last scene, when Macbeth is killed and Malcolm becomes king? Do we see this as the intervention of a divine providence, a restoration of goodness after all the evil? Or do we see little evidence of divine providence and instead signs that the whole cycle of violence and murder could be about to begin all over again? And what does the play really tell us about good and evil? This book sets out to answer these questions, and to show how it is only in recent years that the extent of Shakespeare's achievement in *Macbeth*, and the nature of his vision in the play, has really been grasped.

A summary of the plot

Act One

The play opens in thunder and lightning with Three Witches chanting round a boiling cauldron. A wounded sergeant reports to King Duncan that his generals – Macbeth and Banquo – have defeated the allied forces of Norway and Ireland, led by the traitor Macdonwald. Macbeth and Banquo, wandering on a heath after their victory, meet the Three Witches, who greet them with prophecies. The first witch hails Macbeth as "Thane of Glamis" (his title), the second as "Thane of Cawdor"; the third proclaims he shall "be King hereafter". The witches tell Banquo he will father a line of kings. When they vanish, a messenger arrives from the King, informing Macbeth he is now to be Thane of Cawdor. Macbeth begins to ponder how he can achieve the final prophecy, and become King. When Duncan arrives to stay at the Macbeths' castle at Inverness, Lady Macbeth hatches a plan to murder him and secure the throne for her husband. Macbeth agonises, but Lady Macbeth eventually persuades him.

Act Two

Macbeth hallucinates before entering Duncan's quarters to commit the murder, believing he sees a bloody dagger. After the murder he is so shaken

that Lady Macbeth takes charge, framing
Duncan's sleeping servants, as she has planned
to do, by placing bloody daggers in their hands.
The next morning, Macduff arrives and discovers
Duncan's corpse. Feigning anger, Macbeth
murders the guards before they can protest their
innocence. Macduff is suspicious of Macbeth,
but does not reveal his suspicions publicly.
Fearing for their lives, Duncan's sons flee,
Malcolm to England, Donalbain to Ireland.
Macbeth assumes the throne after being elected
the new King of Scotland.

Act Three

Macbeth is uneasy about Banquo, and the
witches' prophecy which predicts he will father
a line of kings. He hires two men to kill Banquo
and his young son, Fleance. The assassins
succeed in killing Banquo, but Fleance escapes. At
a royal banquet afterwards, Banquo's ghost enters
and sits in Macbeth's place. Macbeth flies into a
rage; a desperate Lady Macbeth tells her guests
that her husband is unwell. The ghost departs but
when he returns a second time, prompting another
display of anger from Macbeth, the thanes flee.

Act Four

Macbeth visits the Three Witches again. They
conjure up spirits: an armed head warns him to
"beware Macduff"; another spirit, a bloody child,

says "none of woman born/ shall harm Macbeth";
a third, a crowned child, says Macbeth will "never
vanquish'd be until/Great Birnam Wood to high
Dunsinane Hill/shall come against him". Macbeth
is told by Lennox, one of the Scottish nobles, that
Macduff is in exile in England. Despite this, he
sends murderers to Macduff's castle where they
kill Macduff's wife and their young son. In the
long, so-called English scene, Macduff (as yet
ignorant of the deaths) is tested by Malcolm, who
is finally convinced of his "truth and honour".
Immediately after this, Macduff learns that his
wife and son have been murdered.

Act Five
Lady Macbeth, now wracked with guilt,
sleepwalks, trying to wash imaginary bloodstains
from her hands. As the English army approaches,
led by Malcolm, Macbeth learns that many of his
thanes are deserting him. While encamped in
Birnam Wood, the English soldiers are ordered to
cut down branches from trees and to carry them as
camouflage, fulfilling the witches' prophecy.
Macbeth delivers a final despairing soliloquy on
learning that his wife has died. (The cause is
undisclosed but Malcolm later suggests she has
committed suicide.)

   In the ensuing battle, Macbeth confronts
Macduff, saying that he cannot be killed by any
man born of woman. But Macduff declares that he

was "from his mother's womb/ Untimely ripp'd".
Macduff beheads Macbeth offstage and the play
ends with Malcom accepting the throne.

THE CHARACTERS

DUNCAN, King of Scotland

MALCOLM, Duncan's son

DONALBAIN, Duncan's son

MACBETH, a general in the King's army, later king

BANQUO, a general

MACDUFF, LENNOX, ROSS, MENTEITH,

ANGUS, CAITHNESS, nobleman of Scotland

FLEANCE, Banquo's son

SIWARD, Earl of Northumberland

YOUNG SIWARD, Siward's son

SETON, personal officer to Macbeth

MACDUFF'S SON

LADY MACBETH

LADY MACDUFF

*An English Doctor, A Scottish Doctor, A Sergeant, A Porter,
An Old Man, Three Murderers, A Lady-in-waiting, Three
Witches, Hecate, Apparitions, Lords, Gentlemen, Officers,
Soldiers, Attendants and Messengers*

What is *Macbeth* about?

The orthodox or traditional idea is that *Macbeth* is not only a study of "ambition" but a study of "evil". The director Peter Hall described it in a 1970 interview as "the most thorough-going study of evil that I know in dramatic literature":

> Evil in every sense: cosmic sickness, personal sickness, personal neurosis, the consequence of sin, the experience of sin, blood leading to more blood, and that, in a way, leading inevitably to regeneration. Disease or crime, or evil, induces death, which induces life. Macbeth presents this cycle of living and, in that sense, I find it the most metaphysical of Shakespeare's plays – an unblinking look at the nature of evil in the person and in the state, and in the cosmos.

One would naturally expect such a play to be terrifying, but in the kind of "cycle" Hall so eloquently describes there is light at the end of the terrible tunnel. Evil "induces death, which induces life" and leads "inevitably to regeneration" and a providential restoration of "Order" – the order that Macbeth destroyed by killing Duncan, the 'Holy King'.

Through most of the 20th century, the dominant view concurred with Sir Peter Hall's: the play's terrors, while alarming, are safely contained;

Evil is finally exorcized by the triumph of Good. This idea of a reassuringly inevitable or providential intervention was rather like, or all too like, Victor Hugo's Romantic view of the reasons for Napoleon's downfall:

> The moment had come for supreme incorruptible justice to intervene... Napoleon had been denounced in infinity, and his fall had been decided. He was in God's way.

Here it's worth recalling two accounts of *Macbeth* that impressed me when I was a schoolboy. One is John Danby's book, *Shakespeare's Doctrine of Nature* (1949), in which Danby compares the "formal outline" of *Macbeth* to the shape of the young Shakespeare's first historical tetralogy – the three Parts of *Henry VI*, and *Richard III*. In this sequence of plays, says Danby, a Holy King is killed by a murderer who is then forced to rule "with blood and iron, proceeding from enormity to enormity", until, finally, "the powers of outraged pity and justice" return to overthrow the murderer. Danby's assumption is that *Macbeth* has a similar moral and even religious framework, a framework in which, once again, "the powers of pity and justice" come out on top, this time in a triumphal last scene in which Macbeth is killed, his forces are routed and Malcolm succeeds to the throne.

L.C. Knights's earlier and very influential account of *Macbeth* in *Explorations* (1946) went even further in insisting on the firmness of the play's "positive values". For Knights, the "main theme of the reversal of values is given out simply and clearly in the first scene — 'fair is foul and foul is fair'; and with it are associated premonitions of the conflict, disorder and moral darkness into which Macbeth will plunge himself". But this situation was, to borrow the Viennese saying, "desperate but not serious", since the disorder and darkness were safely contained. "Well before the end of the first act," Knights assures us, we are "in possession" of those "positive values against which the Macbeth evil will be defined".

Knights writes as though these "positive values" are not only there "in" the play, as part of what we are to suppose people at that time all believed, in a world we have lost: they are also grounded in the inherent structure of reality in the world we all inhabit.

It is only in the last 50 years or so that critics have seriously begun to challenge the sort of positive, providentialist view of *Macbeth* espoused by critics like Danby, Knights and, up to a point at least, Peter Hall. In his pioneering 1963 essay on "The 'Strong Pessimism' of *Macbeth*", Wilbur Sanders protested against all those "readings of *Macbeth* in which evil is somehow subordinated to the good and to the natural, and the military victory of Malcolm's forces is seen as the elimination of the Macbeth-evil": "this kind of simplification", Sanders observed, "domesticates the play and draws its teeth". In another, not so early but resonant 1980 essay that was reprinted in his magnificent collection *Making Trifles of Terrors*, Harry Berger Jr. protested that the natural or even sacred "Order" that provided the assumptive basis for providentialist readings was not conspicuously present – or was nowhere to be found – in the play's opening scenes. Arthur Kinney echoed this protest at the start of his book *Lies Like Truth* (2001).

The opening scenes, after all, are capable of a much more alarming interpretation than traditional critics allow. Take the sinister couplet that concludes the unforgettable but astonishingly brief (15 line) first scene:

> *Fair is foul, and foul is fair,*
> *Hover through the fog and filthy air –*

Providentialists take the witches's words to mean that we are about to witness a reversal or inversion of ordered Nature, where all we need to do, as in Ben Jonson's *Volpone*, is turn things the right way up and order will be restored. But the more alarming possibility is that the witches are mocking or repudiating the very idea of some ontological and moral difference between "fair" and "foul" – and suggesting there is no absolute difference between them, indeed that there are no absolute values at all.

Moments earlier, the witches say they had determined to meet Macbeth

When the hurly-burly's done,
When the battle's lost and won.

Again, we can rationalize the reference to "When the battle's lost and won": the winner's victory will be the opponent's loss. But again there is another, more frightening possibility: that winning is really just losing more slowly – an interpretation that anticipates Macbeth's final nihilistic vision of life itself as a tale "Told by an idiot": "Full of sound

SUPERNATURAL POWERS

The witches' oracular predictions to Macbeth come true, and of course they know where and when to find him. That some of their prophecies to Banquo still haven't been confirmed when the play ends contributes to the uneasiness in the final scene: where, Bertolt Brecht wanted to know, is Fleance? We expect prophecies and predictions in works of art to come true, like the Soothsayer's prediction in *Julius Caesar*, that is usually why they are there. So we shouldn't conclude too quickly that the Weird Sisters must be "real" witches, and therefore must be instruments of Satan, and

and fury" but "Signifying nothing". In this interpretation, the moral categories – Knights's "positive values", and all distinctions between fair and foul, or good and evil, or losing and winning – threaten to disappear into the "fog and filthy air".

In the light of this, it is unsurprising that Lafew's deeply sceptical remarks in *All's Well That Ends Well* about how fragile our assumptions are and how little we know of the world have been cited more than once as appropriate to the mood of *Macbeth*:

> *They say miracles are past; and we have our philosophical persons, to make modern and familiar, things supernatural and causeless.*

that the Christian God must therefore be in his Heaven, so that all may soon be well.

References to the supernatural are more frequent in *Macbeth* than in any other Shakespeare play except *Julius Caesar*. Banquo appeals to the "merciful powers" to "Restrain in me the cursèd thoughts that nature/ Gives way to in repose"; but he doesn't know how strong these powers are, and he is afraid to go to sleep. Lady Macbeth appeals to the "spirits" that "tend on mortal thoughts" to "unsex me here", but we don't know whether these spirits come when they are called; in that case the actress and director have to decide whether to suggest that there is some immediate, fatal tranformation. In this play, the "powers" that appear to be ranged against each other in the opposed worlds of Day and Night remain mysterious and uncertain.◆

Hence is it that we make trifles of terrors, ensconsing ourselves into seeming knowledge, when we should submit ourselves to an unknown fear.

These words provided Wilbur Sanders with an epitaph for his essay "An unknown fear" and Harry Berger with the title for his book (*Making Trifles of Terrors*). Set Lafew's humbling fear of how little we know – or Hamlet's "There are more things in heaven and earth, Horatio, than are dreamt of in our philosophy" – against Victor Hugo's flatulent romantic optimism about why Napoleon's downfall was inevitable, and you have a pretty good idea of the gulf between modern and traditional views of *Macbeth*.

Nor is our attitude to the central character as straightforward as many critics would have us believe. Although we witness his terrible degeneration, he is also the most sensitive and sympathetic character in the play. In L.C. Knights's providentialist view, we "see through" Macbeth in much the same way that we see through a confidence trickster, or a bad argument: he becomes a tyrant who shrinks in stature during the play. Yet we also "see through" him in quite a different sense, seeing his world through his eyes, through his asides and soliloquies, his tortured

Opposite: poster for Orson Welles's 1948 film

CHARLES K. FELDMAN presents
ORSON WELLES
in
MACBETH
by WILLIAM SHAKESPEARE
INTRODUCING
JEANETTE NOLAN
WITH
DAN O'HERLIHY · RODDY McDOWALL · EDGAR BARRIER · ALAN NAPIER

sense that "Nothing is, but what is not" and – this had better be said too –his sometimes astonishingly difficult language. For in a much more alarming way he actually *grows* in stature: the Macbeth we see in the earliest scenes is a nervous wreck who becomes ever more fearless in the fascinated way he watches and reports on his own terrible inner transformation. As Stephen Booth puts it in one of the finest discussions of this play, "to be audience to *Macbeth* is virtually to *be* Macbeth for the duration of the performance". The tragedy, Booth suggests, occurs not so much on stage as "in the audience"; Shakespeare makes us join our minds to Macbeth's both in "his [Macbeth's] sensitive awareness of evil and his practice of it".

Despite the horror we feel for his increasingly monstrous behaviour, we find ourselves forced to admire as well as to condemn his extraordinary vitality and daring. He is a force of nature and, as Wilbur Sanders suggests, his defiant energy represents, even exemplifies, something which Nietsche and D. H. Lawrence both took to be a vital and essential element of human existence.

It is as if the Shakespeare who knew that the meek must, and do, inherit the earth, also saw from a different point of view (Nietzschean, Lawrencian) what a disaster it would be for the earth if they did, and preserved at the very core of his conception of evil an awareness of dynamism and power.

Sanders goes on to quote Henry V:

> *There is some soul of goodness in things evil*
> *Would men observingly distil it out.*

Macbeth is an unsettling play. It is unsettling in the way we are made to see its central figure both as a villain who commits horrifying deeds but also as a hero who compels our admiration. And it is unsettling because it not only suggests that evil is a stronger force than good but questions the whole idea of some absolute standard of goodness against which everything can be measured. Like *King Lear*, it confronts the possibility that we live in an unaccommodating universe where the very idea of external "order" is an illusion. This is a play, to adapt the bleeding captain's words in the second scene, where "discomfort" keeps "swelling" from every "seeming comfort", and the "multiplying villainies of Nature" seem omnipresent and ready to swarm through any breach.

How does Shakespeare create an atmosphere of evil?

What bears in on us in the opening scenes of *Macbeth* is something terrifyingly inchoate. A. P. Rossiter, usually a scrupulously attentive critic, refers to the "breakdown of ordered nature" which is "released by Duncan's murder", but what on earth does he mean? How can he speak of a "breakdown" which is only "released" in the second act, when the play (after its short prologue) starts with with the description of a bloody battle – described as "another Golgotha" (massacre) – in which Nature's "multiplying villainies" are already "swarming"?

And when, once Duncan's murder has taken place, Macbeth reflects that he might be better off dead, his miniature sketch of Duncan's reign scarcely suggests that it was a period of peace and order:

> *After life's fitful fever he sleeps well,*
> *Treason has done his worst; nor steel, nor poison,*
> *Malice domestic, foreign levy, nothing,*
> *Can touch him further. [3.2]*

What is so disturbing about Act One is not the sense of evil events disrupting a stable, morally clear world but the *absence* of any such world. The atmosphere of the opening scenes is one of continual "Hurly-burly", where "fair is foule and foule is fair" – words spoken by the witches and then eerily echoed by Macbeth when he first appears. As Arthur Kinney points out in *Lies Like Truth*, the first four scenes all begin with questions: "When shall we three meete again?"; "What bloody man is that?"; "Where has thou beene, sister?"; "Is execution done on Cawdor?" and the play thereafter resounds with questions: "If we should faile?"; "Is this a Dagger, which I see before me...?"; "But wherefore could I not pronounce Amen?"

The questions help establish the play's unsettling atmosphere, as do the tales and acts of violence, threats, hallucinations, charms, conjurations and secret plotting. *Macbeth* is a "play of conspiracies", says Kinney; from the first scene when the witches conspire with each other we have one conspiracy after another:

> of Macbeth and the witches with their foreseen titles; of Macbeth and his wife; of Macbeth and Banquo complicit in silence; of Macbeth and Lennox, who supports his story at the discovery in silence; of Macbeth and Ross as he interrogates others and discovers Macduff's flight.

The play is full, too, of rumours and mysteries.

"Surprise is continual," writes G. Wilson Knight:

> Macbeth does not understand how he can be Thane of Cawdor (1.3). Lady Macbeth is startled at the news of Duncan's visit (1.5); Duncan at the fact of Macbeth's arrival before himself (1.6). There is the general amazement at the murder; of Lennox, Ross and the Old Man at the strange happenings in earth and heaven on the night of the murder (2.3; 2.4). Banquo and Fleance are unsure of the hour (2.1). No one is sure of Macduff's mysterious movements. Lady Macbeth is baffled by Macbeth's enigmatic hints as to the "deed of dreadful note" (3.2). The two murderers are not certain as to whom has wronged them, Macbeth or Banquo (3.1); they do not understand the advent of the "third murderer" (3.3). Ross and Lady Macduff are at a loss as to Macduff's flight, and warning is brought to Lady Macduff by a mysterious messenger who "is not by her known" (4.2). Malcolm suspects Macduff, and there is a long dialogue due to his "doubts" (4.3); and in the same scene Malcolm recognizes Ross as his countryman yet strangely "knows him not" (4.3).

The questions and the mysteries reinforce the sense of a lack of order and the contradictory impressions the play produces in us which make us feel that

...we feare, yet know not what we feare,
But floate upon a wilde and violent Sea
Each way, and none. [4.2]

Following the witches on the heath, the play's
second scene gives us our first real sense of the
situation from which the play's events will unfold.
We hear from the Captain his description of the
battle in which Macbeth fights Macdonwald. The
"brave" and (for now) good Macbeth defeats and
kills the "mercilesse" and bad Macdonwald, but, as
has often been remarked, the Captain's description
of a "doubtful" conflict between "two spent
Swimmers" who "cling together,/And choake their
Art" makes the two men seem indistinguishable,
while the Captain's attempt to provide a
distinction by calling one "mercilesse" and the
other "brave" is itself exposed by the
interchangeability of the adjectives: it is hard to
think the unseamer more merciful than the man
he unseams.

> *Doubtful it stood,*
> *As two spent swimmers that do cling together*
> *And choke their art. The merciless Macdonwald*
> *(Worthy to be a rebel, for to that*
> *The multiplying villainies of nature*
> *Do swarm upon him) from the Western Isles*
> *Of kerns and gallowglasses is supplied;*
> *And Fortune, on his damned quarrel smiling,*

Showed like a rebel's whore. But all's too weak:
For brave Macbeth (well he deserves that name),
Disdaining Fortune, with his brandished steel,
Which smoked with bloody execution,
Like valor's minion carved out his passage
Till he faced the slave;
Which ne'er shook hands nor bade farewell to
                                                              him
Till he unseamed him from the nave to th' chops
And fixed his head upon our battlements. [1.2]

As the American critic Stephen Booth has pointed out in a brilliant analysis of this speech in *King Lear, Macbeth, Indefinition and Tragedy,* Macbeth comes across as "impersonal, ruthless and violent"; he may be "the defender of right" but he sounds "more a monster of cruelty than Macdonwald does". Throughout the Captain's narrative, indeed, "the doers of good sound either like or worse than the evildoers". And what is true of the Captain's narrative is true of the play as a whole: the sense of evil always seems much stronger to us than the sense of good. The outcome of the "doubtful" conflicts described appears to depend on chance and Macbeth's Might, not on Right, or any providential power.

Is Macbeth the plaything of a giant malevolence?

The first mystery in this play full of mysteries is, of course, the nature of the witches. Who are they? Are they natural or supernatural, real or imaginary? In a sense, as Stephen Booth observes, they are more real to us than anyone else in the play because they are the first characters we meet. In effect, we see all the subsequent action through their prophecies to Macbeth (that he will become Thane of Cawdor, then King of Scotland) and Banquo (that his children will become kings).

In trying to understand who they are, Banquo's amazed response when he first sees them is important:

> What are these,
> So withered, and so wild in their attire,
> That look not like th'inhabitants o'th'earth
> And yet are on't? [1.3]

Banquo then addresses and questions the strange creatures, while providing further descriptive details:

> Live you, or are you aught
> That man may question? You seem to
> understand me,

By each at once her choppy finger laying
Upon her skinny lips. You should be women,
And yet your beards forbid me to interpret
That you are so.

Macbeth himself then asks, more crisply: "Speak if you can: what are you?" In the period after the Restoration when the witches were routinely trivialised and often wore conical hats, this question would have seemed stupid rather than troubled. But Shakespeare's witches are more mysterious, more frighteningly ambivalent.

As the respected actor, director, critic and dramatist Harley Granville-Barker noted in his *Prefaces to Shakespeare* (1927-54), the witches are never actually *called* witches in the play. They are called the Weird Sisters. A.C. Bradley always referred to them as witches, though he insisted that they are not, "in any sense whatever, supernatural beings": "They are old women, poor and ragged, skinny and hideous, full of vulgar spite, occupied in killing their neighbours' swine or revenging themselves on sailors' wives who have refused them chestnuts", although they are also "instruments of darkness" who "have received from evil spirits certain supernatural powers".

Many contemporary critics, however, prefer to follow Granville-Barker – and the play – by calling them the Weird Sisters, and

A.D. Nuttall explained why in his last book, *Shakespeare the Thinker* (2007):

Weird or wyrd in Old English means "fate." The sisters are three in number like the classical Fates [or "Parcae"]. At the same time they are witches, a relatively familiar feature of the rural social scene.

In the village on the Welsh border where I lived as a child we had a "cunning woman" who had spells and simples, written out in a Herefordshire Country Council school exercise book, for curing various ailments, animal or human. The community never rose against her, but one could imagine it happening (should a cow die, say, after

PERSECUTING WITCHES

"Thou shalt not suffer a witch to live" (*Exodus*, 22.18): the Bible tells us not only that witches exist, but that they must be hunted down and destroyed. And yet, in the so-called Dark Ages, this clear Biblical injunction was neglected. In the eighth century St Boniface went so far as to declare that it was unChristian to believe in witches or werewolves, and the Emperor Charlemagne ordered that those who burnt witches should be put to death themselves. St Ageland's ruling, in the ninth century, that anybody who believed in witches was "beyond doubt an infidel and a pagan" entered canon law in the *Canon Episcopi* or receiving her medicine). The Weird Sisters are not grand, as the Fates are. They belong to a northern, Breughelesque world of cooking pots and greasy kitchen scraps.

Nuttall writes wonderfully of what he calls the "primitive, twilit stuff" in *Macbeth*, and that might remind us of one way in which the play represented a new departure. With the exception of *King Lear*, the recently preceding plays – including the "problem" comedies – presented highly evolved, sometimes "over-ripe" societies, while *Macbeth* presents a historically primitive, 11th-century world.

The identity of the witches in this primitive world is never clear. If they are instruments of

---

Capitulum Episcopi. Burning witches was expressly forbidden. The many murderous outbreaks and burnings, when witches were scapegoated as well as Jews, remained local affairs not a divinely ordained duty. This changed when the Age of Enlightenment finally dawned.

In 1484 Pope Innocent VIII's *Witch Bull* provided Dominican monks and inquisitors with the general mandate they longed for.

After that, the holy Inquisition had its licence to torture and kill witches as well as Jews and heretics. Protestant reformers like the ex-Dominican Luther in Germany, Calvin in Geneva, or Zwingli in Zurich, were no less eager to do their Christian duty. The European Witch Craze went on for two centuries, before it finally and rather mysteriously died out.

By the end of the 16th century there was still

Satan – as Banquo supposes when he exclaims, after their first prophesy is fulfilled: "What, can the devil speak true?" – then this suggests that the world of the play is a Christian one, but as Nuttall suggests, they seem curiously capricious and infantile for traditional witches – hardly less concerned with the pilots and chestnuts they discuss in the third scene than with Macbeth and Scotland.

Yet precisely what the witches are and are not – a question which can never be resolved – is less interesting than why they are there, and what they and their predictions tell us about Macbeth, and about the nature of nature, or reality – a preoccupation which is closely bound up, in the play, with the question of free will.

Is Macbeth a free agent, or is he from the very

---

widespread belief in witches. At one end of the spectrum were illiterate and superstitious villagers: some poor farmer whose only cow had suddenly died or who was impotent on his wedding night would blame the poor old biddy who collected herbs and dispensed potions. But at the other end were great Renaissance thinkers like Jean Bodin or Justus Lipsius.

A few great thinkers like Erasmus, whom Shakespeare first read as a schoolboy in Stratford, remained quiet about the question of witchcraft; in his momentous *Commentaries on the New Testament*, Erasmus refrained from comment at every point that was relevant to the witch-craze. Montaigne, one of Shakespeare's favourite writers, never went so riskily far as to deny that witches exist, but questioned our mental capacity to know who is or is not a witch.◆

beginning, in Wilbur Sanders's phrase, "the plaything of a giant malevolence"?

Macbeth's attitude to the witches's prophecies is unstable and uncertain; nor is it clear what, if anything, the witches implant in his mind. There is a sense in which Macbeth confers on the prophecy of his becoming king "all the reality it possesses" – in other words, it is a guide to what he should do, no more – but there is another sense in which he is "the slave of the prophecy" (and therefore has no free will at all). This "doubleness", writes Sanders in *The Dramatist and the Received Idea*, a searching critical discussion of the play,

> is characteristic of all the predictions and fulfilments in the play – they are both powerless to alter the course of events, and they reflect faithfully the course of events which is unalterable. The very predictions seem to presuppose the effect they will have upon Macbeth – as if a deterministic net had been cast over the whole action. Yet Macbeth proceeds, with every appearance of freedom, to draw the *un*necessary conclusion from the prophecies: that chance will *not* crown him without a stir. And even that conclusion is presupposed by the prophecy, since a Macbeth who did not stir would have become the vassal of heir-apparent Malcolm, Prince of Cumberland.

How sympathetic do we feel to Macbeth?

If *Macbeth* raises disturbing questions about the nature of nature, and the existence of free will, there is at least one sense in which it is also a profoundly Christian play. Macbeth has a Christian sensitivity, and though he tries hard to reject them, the values he has been brought up to believe in are Christian values.

Unlike the men he sends to butcher Banquo, whom no one supposes will be tortured by remorse, Macbeth has a conscience. But then, as he reflects with a grim contempt that is already brimming over with fears of his *own* remorse, these murderers "go for men" only "in the catalogue" – i.e. barely count as human beings. Macbeth, however, suffers agonies because of his nature. In her first soliloquy in the fifth scene, Lady Macbeth fears the way in which whatever her husband would have "highly" he wants to have "holily" – since in her pragmatic view (which has its own deranged "catalogue") her husband is "too full o' the' milk of human kindness".

In his own first soliloquy in the seventh scene, Macbeth asserts his readiness to "jump the life to come" – to forfeit his place in the afterlife – if only he can safely get what he wants in this world. But he is deceiving himself. In the last part of the same soliloquy the conscience he wants to suppress erupts; he can't help thinking what the reaction will be to Duncan's death, and his prodigious imagination provides the vision of how

> *pity, like a naked new-born babe,*
> *Striding the blast, or Heaven's cherubim horsed*
> *Upon the sightless couriers of the air,*
> *Shall blow the horrid deed in every eye,*
> *That tears shall drown the wind. [1.7]*

Macbeth tries once again to repress his Christian

BABES

Macbeth, says the critic Michael Long, is "the great play of babes".

* Lady Macbeth in effect commits the first atrocities of the play when she summons infernal powers to "unsex her" and boasts of her ability to dash out a baby's brains.

* Banquo figures as a source of babes: he will "get" kings, his "children shall be kings"; he will be "root and father" to a line of kings.

* When Macduff later replaces Banquo as a father, we hear of his "babes"; "your little ones"; his tiny, impudently plucky "egg"; his "young fry. When he hears of their slaughter his mind is overwhelmed by "children...babes...pretty ones...pretty chickens" and on the battlefield he is haunted by "my... children's ghosts".

* Duncan is a father too: he names his son his heir. So

feelings at the end of the climactic banquet scene in Act Three, when he says that

> *Strange things I have in head, that will to hand,*
> *Which must be acted, ere they may be scanned.*
> *[3.4]*

He now thinks he can take thought out of the equation entirely, and simply act. But once again he is wrong: he never knows his own deepest (or religious with a small r) impulses in the way that

is Siward, whose son dies at the end.

* Macbeth feels humiliated by the fact that he is no more than "the baby of a girl", while Lady Macbeth talks scornfully of "the eye of childhood" which hardened killers are better without.

* In Act Four, Scene One, one of the ingredients for the witches' cauldron is the finger of a "birth-strangled babe", while two of the three apparitions they summon up for Macbeth are children.

* Macbeth finally comes to know the worst when Macduff tells him

he was not "born of woman" but was from his "mother's womb/ Untimely ripp'd".

The babe, says Cleanth Brooks in his famous essay, 'The Naked Babe', "is perhaps the most powerful symbol in the tragedy". The witches prophesy that Macbeth is to have the crown, but that the crown will pass to Banquo's children. Shakespeare points up Macbeth's motivation for murdering Banquo very carefully:

> *Then prophet-like,*
> *They hail'd him father to a line*
> *of kings.*
> *Upon my head they plac'd a*

his wife does. By Act Five, Scene Three, however, he has come to understand that he has been doomed by his choices and can never expect or "look to have" – "highly" or "holily" –

> *that which should accompany old age,*
> *As honour, love, obesience, troops of friends.*

In his momentous letter to his wife he had addressed her as his "dearest partner of greatness", but when he loses her in Act Five he is so "sick at

> *fruitless crown,*
> *And put a barren sceptre in*
> *my gripe,*
> *Thence to be wrench'd with*
> *an unlineal hand,*
> *No son of mine succeeding.*
> *[3.1]*

There is resentment against Banquo because Banquo – who, says Brooks, has "risked nothing, who has remained upright" – will have kings for children. Macbeth will not. Yet while Banquo is murdered, Fleance escapes. Macbeth's attempt to control the future fails. It is altogether appropriate, says Brooks, that when Macbeth returns to the witches for counsel,

two of the apparitions they reveal are babes, the crowned babe and the bloody babe.

For the babe signifies the future which Macbeth would control and cannot control. It is the unpredictable thing itself – as Yeats has put it magnificently, "The uncontrollable mystery on the bestial floor".

Macbeth's distraught mind thus forces him to make war on children, but it is a hopeless war. When Macduff's son, in his helplessness, defies his murderers, his defiance "testifies to the force which threatens Macbeth and which Macbeth heart" that he cannot even mourn or grieve.

This brings home the relevance of a distinction that Erich Auerbach made in *Mimesis: The Representation of Reality in Western Literature* (1946). In this extraordinary book, which ranges from Homer to Proust and is one of the few very great works of literary criticism, Auerbach distinguishes between the classical and the Christian view of tragedy. Whereas in the former, characters are able to view themselves, and their emotions and actions, with an almost icy

---

cannot destroy".

But the babe signifies not only the future: it symbolizes, too, everything which gives life meaning and "all those emotional and – to Lady Macbeth – irrational ties which make man... human". Take the passage in Act One, Scene Seven where Macbeth compares the pity for his victim-to-be, Duncan, to

> *a naked new-born babe,*
> *Striding the blast, or*
> *Heaven's cherubim, hors'd*
> *Upon the sightless couriers*
> *of the air...*

Pity is being compared to a naked babe, the most sensitive and helpless thing,

yet, as Brooks notes, no sooner has the comparison been made than the symbol of weakness begins to turn into a symbol of strength: the babe is pictured "Striding the blast". Pity, it is suggested, is both helpless and powerful: it is strong, says Brooks, "because of its very weakness.

The paradox is inherent in the situation itself; and it is the paradox that will desroy the over-brittle rationalism on which Macbeth founds his career." Babies are tender and vulnerable, yet they symbolize, in Macbeth, what is creative and indestructible in the future.◆

35

objectivity, in the latter they are quite incapable of detaching themselves in this manner.

In considering St Augustine, for example, Auerbach notes that the "urgently impulsive element in his character makes it impossible for him to accommodate himself to the comparatively cool and rational procedure of the classical, and specifically of the Roman, style, which looks at and organises things from above".

When Racine's Phèdre, on the other hand, reports on her own inner tumult, she is somehow detached from it; her language always suggests that she sees it, as it were, "from above", albeit with terrifying lucidity. The greatest French tragedy, in Auerbach's sense, is classical. But the greatest English tragedy is Christian. There is no classical certainty or assurance about Macbeth; he is unable to analyze his situation with the coolness and absence of emotion of a Phèdre. The convulsive, eruptive processes of his tortured imagination are apprehended far more helplessly, from within.

Macbeth's own Christian, decidedly unclassical and unSenecan, radically *inward*-looking character corresponds with the sense of the psyche as something stratified, or terrifyingly vertiginous, which Auerbach analyses in Augustine and which is so conspicuous in the poetry of Gerard Manley Hopkins – the sense, or idea, that the mind can fall (like Milton's Satan or Dostoevsky's Raskolnikov) in the most sudden and precipitate way, from goodness into utter wickedness:

> *O, the mind, mind has mountains; cliffs of fall*
> *Frightful, sheer, no-man-fathomed. Hold them*
> *cheap*
> *May who ne'er hung there. Nor does long our*
> *small*
> *Durance deal with that steep or deep. Here!*
> *creep,*
> *Wretch, under a comfort serves in a whirlwind:*
> *all*
> *Life death does end and each days dies with*
> *sleep.*

Macbeth's mind has its own "cliffs of fall", as we begin to see in the middle of the play's first act. When Duncan announces his decision to invest his elder son Malcolm as Prince of Cumberland, in other words his successor, Macbeth immediately registers his utter consternation. He is no fool, but he had never anticipated this and says, in an aside:

> *The Prince of Cumberland! That is a step*
> *On which I must fall down, or else o'erleap,*
> *For in my way it lies. Stars, hide your fires;*
> *Let not light see my black and deep desires:*
> *The eye wink at the hand; yet let that be*
> *Which the eye fears, when it is done, to see. [1.4]*

"Done" is a terribly significant word in this play, since one of its underlying themes is that what is done cannot be undone, and Macbeth's great first soliloquy three scenes later begins with with a threefold play on the word. In his soliloquy he is picking up from where he left off, still brooding on Duncan's decision.

The soliloquy begins with the little but powerful word "If", which then controls all of the verb tenses throughout the long and tremendous first sentence (see opposite). The edgily uncertain verbs like *could* and *might* and *would* follow from that "If", which grammarians call a "logical constant". Indeed, a logically directed movement or trajectory can be followed through the whole soliloquy, which is in one sense entirely concerned with what is expedient or prudent. The "If" carries – or answers to – Macbeth's terrible fear that if or when the deed is "done" it will *not* be done or over with or, as we also say, done with: it *will* have consequences, that he will not be able to prevent or control, and what is done cannot be undone. Macbeth struggles to stifle that fear.

Something else, however – some terrible compulsion that has little to do with logic or pragmatic calculation, or trying to think like a moral gangster – is also at work, so that the soliloquy follows two very different trajectories of thought and feeling. The first of these (which we have been examining) is the trajectory of logic.

Thickening up of the language with these Latinate polysyllabic words after the previous short ones suggests Macbeth's doubts. "Trammel" is an invented word: a trammeled or hobbled horse is tied to nothing but itself.

The faltering rhythms of the speech reflect Macbeth's state of mind: note the twitchy repeated double "ifs" and "buts"

Effect of the speech reinforced by the confusing echo of "'twere", "'tis" and "it were"

If it 'twere done, when 'tis done, then 'twere well

*It were done quickly: if th'*assassination

Could trammel up *the consequence, and catch*

With his surcease, success; that but this blow

Might be the be-all and the end-all – here,

But here, *upon this bank and shoal of time,*

We'd jump the life to come.

Note the breathy urgency of this, with the repetition of "here"

Pronouncing this difficult phrase out loud involves the actor in the speech's faltering rhythm

The soliloquy ends by considering, again, an idea which he has considered in his earlier aside, the idea of a catastrophic jump, an utterly fatal "o'releap":

> *I have no spur*
> *To prick the sides of my intent, but only*
> *Vaulting ambition, which o'erleaps itself*
> *And falls on th'other*

This, we might say – the belief that he mustn't murder Duncan – is the logical point or conclusion of this crucial soliloquy, although, like Hamlet's most famous soliloquy, it doesn't arrive at a formal conclusion but stops when it is interrupted. In the case of the earlier tragedy, Hamlet spots Ophelia. In this case Lady Macbeth enters, interrupting the soliloquy's final sentence. But the *logical* conclusion to Macbeth's soliloquy, unlike Hamlet's, is already clear, and he tells his wife what it is: "We will proceed no further in this business": he must not do the deed.

But if one trajectory of this soliloquy is logical, the other trajectory is not. In this, Macbeth seems to feel he can only get the "horrid image" conjured up by the Weird Sisters out of his mind by releasing "it" into the world and giving it birth, in other words by committing the murder and becoming King. Macbeth's wife longs to be her husband's queen, and in better circumstances would have been and relished being a good queen; but in Macbeth's case the wish to be King is never as strong as this desperate wish to exorcize the monster, or "horrid image", that has possessed his mind.

So this great soliloquy and the asides he speaks before it in Act One, Scene Four, show Macbeth's imagination caught like a rat in a trap: there is a constantly thrashing activity that gets nowhere. As A.C. Bradley memorably remarked, Macbeth will commit the deed as though it were some "terrible duty". So the soliloquy moves along two quite different trajectories of thought and feeling, one driven by logic, since he is no fool, the other driven by feeling, or emotional desperation. He longs to be able to say: "It's done." Unable to accept the pitiless and shallow rationalism urged on him by his wife, he is hopelessly caught, as Cleanth Brooks has put it, "between the irrational and the rational".

So he *wants* to think that "th'assassination/ Could trammel up the consequences", but he also doubts that this is possible, and as he doubts it his language seems to thicken or become more opaque: he starts using polysyllabic Latinate words instead of his previously short, largely monosyllabic words with Old English roots. We could suppose that he speaks of an "assassination" because he doesn't want to use the word "murder", like modern military gangsters who use the phrase "terminate with extreme prejudice" when they mean "kill". But according to the *OED*, "assassination" is a new word Shakespeare is inventing.

Neither Macbeth nor Shakespeare is inventing the word "trammel". That word is now unfamiliar to us, like Macbeth's later word "seeling" ("Come, seeling night/ Scarf up the tender eye of pitiful day"), because so few of us raise horses or train falcons. But both words are drawn from the range of outdoor activities that would have been familiar to a Scottish lord: riding, hunting, fishing, falconry.

What makes this use of "trammel" remarkable is that its meaning is ambiguous and its use reflects Macbeth's divided state of mind. If you trammel or net a bird or fish you have caught it, and that is that: "'twere well it were done quickly"! But people also spoke of trammeling or binding the legs of a colt or young horse to stop it from straying, a much trickier and more uncertain activity.*

The verbal complexities of this speech are labyrinthine, and astonish us by seeming beyond the reach of any consciously purposive creative intelligence. Shakespeare has so far sunk himself

---

*The image of an uncontrollable horse reappears at the end of the soliloquy when Macbeth talks of "Heaven's cherubim horsed/ Upon the sightless couriers of the air" – and in the way he associates the horse-pricking "spur" with "vaulting ambition" that "overleaps itself".

into the mindfalls of Macbeth's anguished imagination as to make us intimately involved in its inner workings. His ability to understand what Macbeth feels, and his determination to make us understand it, becomes even clearer if we consider the famous soliloquy in Act Two which follows Duncan's murder.

Why is the relatively uneducated Macbeth's language so difficult?

After he has killed Duncan, and when his wife goes off to place the incriminating daggers beside the sleeping groom, Macbeth is alone for a few moments. In his second, agonised soliloquy ("Whence is that knocking?"), he uses the word "incarnadine". According to *New English Dictionary*, this is the first recorded use of the word: Macbeth is not just using it, he is inventing it, just as he invents the word "assassination".

How is't with me, when every noise appals me?
What hands are here? Ha, they pluck out
                              mine eyes.
Will all great Neptune's ocean wash this blood
Clean from my hand? No – this my hand

> *will rather*
> *The multitudinous seas incarnardine,*
> *Making the green one red. [2.2]*

"Incarnadine" comes, like "incarnation", from the Latin word *caro,* where the genitive is *carnis.* The Latin word means flesh, not blood. Macbeth is suggesting that his bloody hands would turn the seas into flesh, and in this case bleeding flesh. That is an even more horrifying image than the idea that the "multitudinous" waters

THE PORTER

Given that parts of *Macbeth* are often thought to have been written by other hands – some contemporary critics even believe Shakespeare wrote it in collaboration with that most twisted of his peers, the playwright Thomas Middleton – it's not surprising the Porter is a controversial figure. Coleridge, for example, thought the Porter's scene

"disgusting" and "written for the mob by some other hand"; he couldn't believe even "one syllable has the ever-present being of Shakespeare".

This is hard to credit. For one thing, as the critic Kenneth Muir points out, the Porter's appearance has a practical function; the actor playing *Macbeth* would need time to wash his hands and change his clothes between the scene of Duncan's murder and the following scene when he meets with Macduff and Lenox.

Muir also notes how the Porter compares himself to the Porter of Hell-gate who appeared in Medieval would be turned into blood.

This is a good example of what the great Japanese director Tadashi Suzuki had in mind when he suggested that many of Shakespeare's characters would not be able to understand their own speeches. Macbeth is not, like young Hamlet, a polymathic Renaissance prince. He is highly intelligent, but no intellectual; in that respect he could remind us, like James Joyce's Leopold Bloom or D.H. Lawrence's Tom Brangwen, that highly intelligent people are not

---

Mystery Plays, usually connected to Christ's entrance into Hell, and becomes part of the unsettling Christian imagery that runs through Macbeth. "Knocking" itself, as Muir tells us, is also a significant strand of imagery in the play.

Indeed the Porter is central to Shakespeare's purpose. When accused of drunkenness, he launches into a brief speech on the effect of drink. Drink, he says, "provokes the desire, but it takes away the performance". As Muir reminds us: "The contrast between *desire* and *act* is repeated several times in the course of the play." Take, for example, Lady Macbeth's, "Art thou afeard/To be the same in thine own act and valour,/As thou art in desire?" and Macbeth's desire "To crown my thoughts with acts, be it thought and done". In the Porter, Muir suggests, Shakespeare powerfully reinforces our sense of "the paradox and enigma of the nature of man".

But why is the Porter seen as *comic*? The 19th-century intellectual and opium-addict Thomas de Quincey – a friend of Coleridge's – answered this by saying he isn't. He stirs not comic relief but a feeling of "peculiar

always intellectuals and that many intellectuals are not intelligent. He is an extraordinarily fierce and courageous warrior, in this respect more like Coriolanus than Hamlet. Although his metaphors reveal an imaginative intensity that is equal to Hamlet's, their *range* of reference is more reminiscent of the unbookish Claudius, drawn mainly from hunting, fighting and half-remembered scraps of a nursery education.

So what are we to think, when this intensely imaginative but sparsely educated warrior lord

---

awfulness and a depth of solemnity". It is only when the Porter breaks into the sheer horror of the murder scene with his bawdy punning (the only punning in the play, Coleridge shrewdly notes), that the full horror is established. The transience of the scene makes it all the more horrific. In his essay, "On the Knocking at the Gate in *Macbeth*", De Quincey argues that the very *normality* of the Porter scene is what makes it so effective:

> If the reader has ever witnessed a wife, a daughter, or sister in a fainting fit, he may chance to have observed that the most affecting moment in such a spectacle, is that in which a sigh or stirring announce the recommencement of suspended life... he will be aware that at no moment was his sense of the complete suspension and pause in ordinary human concerns so full and affecting, as that moment when the suspension ceases, and the goings on of human life are suddenly resumed.

Not only, de Quincey suggests, does this interlude find its power in the brief resumption of "the goings on of human life", but it also marks the transition point in suddenly uses a difficult word like "incarnadine"? Should we suppose that the fierce warrior Macbeth is a secret reader who can not only use but invent the polysyllabic Latinate word "incarnardine", and can then be no less unexpectedly considerate when he explains what the word means in good old, largely monosyllabic English? Of course not. In poetic-dramatic terms that would be absurd, just as it would be absurd, in musical-dramatic terms, for Verdi's Violetta in *La Traviata* to keep coughing in her final aria because

---

the play. From now on the world of the human gives way to the "world of devils":

> the human has made its reflux upon the fiendish; the pulses of life are beginning to beat again; and the re-establishment of the goings on of the world in which we live first makes us profoundly sensible of the awful parenthesis that has suspended them.

Quite at odds with his friend Coleridge, de Quincey thinks the Porter, rather than reflecting none of Shakespeare's genius, is profound evidence of it. He concludes, rather breathlessly:

O, mighty poet! Thy works are not as those of other men, simply and merely great works of art; but are also like the phenomena of nature, like the sun and the sea, the stars and the flowers, like frost and snow, rain and dew, hail-storm and thunder, which are to be studied with entire submission of our own faculties, and in the perfect faith that in them there can be not too much or too little, nothing useless or inert but that, the further we press in our discoveries, the more we shall see proofs of design and self-supporting arrangement where the careless eye had seen nothing but accident.◆

she is dying of consumption.

The difficult new word "incarnardine" is being invented by Shakespeare, not by Macbeth. Shakespeare, with his unmatched ability to get inside his characters, is representing – or, literally, *re*-presenting – the horror that Macbeth feels when he looks at his bloody hands and realises that what he has done is so momentous, so irreversible. At such a point many great "realist" novelists, from Flaubert to the young James Joyce, might have felt the need to restrict themselves to whatever words might plausibly have been used by the character – be it Flaubert's Emma Bovary or Stephen in Joyce's *Portrait of the Artist as a Young Man,* where each chapter shows how the successive growth in Stephen's vocabulary of words extends the available vocabulary or keyboard of his thoughts and feelings.

But Macbeth's suddenly difficult language represents his inner state of being, not his consciously reflective thoughts. Shakespeare is using the full resources of his own language to convey what is happening inside Macbeth, although the character himself would almost certainly never invent, or even understand, difficult words like "incarnadine". In *Crime and Punishment* Dostoevsky presents Raskolnikov's thoughts and feelings through words we can imagine, or simply assume, the character would use. But in Macbeth's astonishing early soliloquies, what Shakespeare is showing and exploring is the inner state of a man who tries to suppress or deny the promptings of his own nature.

Franz Kafka once observed:

> The longing for the divine, the sense of shame at the violation of holiness which always accompanies it, men's innate demand for justice – these are mighty and invincible forces, which grow stronger as men try to oppose them. They exert a moral control. A criminal must therefore suppress these forces in himself before he can commit an objectively criminal act. For that reason, every crime is preceded by a spiritual violation.

This is interesting because Kafka talks *not* of divinity and justice, but of the human *longing* for the divine and men's innate *demand* for justice. In the same way, Shakespeare's play does not reveal any all-encompassing moral and spiritual order which exists *outside* Macbeth's tortured consciousness. What it does reveal is that Macbeth feels the same forces Kafka talks about – the *longing* for divinity and the *demand* for justice – but tries to suppress them in himself. And the crime he commits in murdering Duncan therefore has to be, as Kafka puts it, "preceded by a spiritual mutilation".

Macbeth's great soliloquy at the end of Act One

testifies to the power of these imaginative needs and moral promptings which "grow stronger" even as he tries to discount them, or see them as unmanly, womanish fictions. This is what Lady Macbeth means when she says "Yet doe I feare thy Nature". Macbeth, as F.R. Leavis and almost every critic who has written on the play remarks, is "fatally ignorant of his nature".

Is Duncan a saintly king?

Duncan the Holy King is what you get if you place a Christian providentialist grid over the play and then report on whatever shows through it. Plenty of critics and directors have, in effect, done just that. Even in Trevor Nunn's superb 1977 production, which was radical in many other respects and is fortunately still available on DVD, Duncan appeared in white robes, with a large cross and light playing like a halo on his saintly white head.

But there is nothing in the play, and nothing in the sources that Shakespeare consulted or those that he didn't, to suggest that Duncan was a pious believer. In this respect the historical Duncan was altogether unlike the historical Macbeth, who made a pilgrimage to Rome – an astonishing thing for an 11th-century king to do – and was probably the last Scottish king to be buried on the sacred isle of Iona.

Holinshed (1529-1580), whose historical *Chronicles* Shakespeare drew on as his main source, presents Duncan II as a weak king, unfit to rule over a divided, pre-feudal country. Even his virtues were, like those of Shakespeare's Henry VI, disabling: he was "so soft and gentle of nature" that his people wished him "more like his cousin Makbeth", who, "if he had not been somewhat cruel of nature, might have been thought more worthy of the government of a realm". Holinshed reports the rebel Macdonwald's scornful view that Duncan was "a fainthearted milksop, more meet to govern a sort of idle monks in some cloister, than to have the rule of such valiant and hardy men of war as the Scots were".

The *Chronicles* also tell us, and told Shakespeare, that Makbeth was "sore troubled" because, while weak, Duncan was also cunning – and did "what in him lay to defraud him [Makbeth] of all manner of title and claim" to the throne.

So did Shakespeare simply eliminate all this from his play? Yes, according to providentialist readings. In the 1951 New Arden edition, Kenneth Muir allows that the historical Macbeth had a "genuine grievance" against Duncan, who by proclaiming his son Prince of Cumberland took away from Macbeth any prospect of the throne. But, says Muir, Shakespeare simply "suppresses these facts", making his Duncan "old and holy" and passing over his reported weaknesses. At the same time, Shakespeare "deliberately blackened the guilt of Macbeth".

Is this really true? I don't think so. The text suggests that, far from simply ignoring Holinshed's assessment, Shakespeare was strongly influenced by it, portraying Duncan as, if not weak exactly, then certainly as most unwarrior-like, yet at the same time crafty and ruthless when it came to defending his own interests.

Apart from Henry VI, Duncan is the only

HISTORICAL INACCURACIES

The most important "historical inaccuracy" resulted from Shakespeare's decision to compress the historical Macbeth's long reign of 17 years into a few months or weeks, and to ignore the long account in Holinshed of the many "good laws" that the historical Macbeth passed and – unlike the "feeble and slothful" Duncan II – enforced during the greater period of his long reign. According to Holinshed, Macbeth killed Duncan in broad daylight, not in hugger-mugger, with Banquo as his chief accomplice; Shakespeare didn't want that, and incorporated details from Holinshed's account of the murder of King Duff, 80 years earlier. Shakespeare's play has Macbeth deciding to murder Banquo and Fleance very soon after his murder of Duncan, although, in Shakespeare's primary historical source, ten years

Shakespearean monarch who does not lead his army into battle. He is *hors de combat*: we first see him as an elderly non-combatant, waiting anxiously on the edge of the battlefield for news of what Banquo and above all Macbeth – the real saviour of Scotland – have accomplished.

His reaction to the Captain's report is curiously bloodless. After hearing how Macbeth "unseamed" the rebel Macdonwald

> *from th'nave to the chops,*
> *And fixed his head upon our battlements, [1.2]*

passed before the historical Macbeth decided to murder the entirely unhistorical Banquo. All of these decisions were deliberate and "artistic". Shakespeare *decided* to fly against the supposedly historical facts in the *Chronicle*. He was writing a tragedy, not a history of Scotland. Such departures from his historical sources are fascinating in critical rather than historical terms, because they allow us to peep into the Shakespearian workshop.

On the other hand Shakespeare could not have known that Banquo and Fleance never existed, historically, or that Macduff didn't kill Macbeth in the battle depicted in the play's final scene. The historical Macbeth escaped from what is called – appropriately enough, after a Scottish festival or myth – the Battle of the Seven Sleepers. He was only killed later, at Lumphanan, and then, for a few months, his adopted son Lulach ruled as "King" in northern Scotland, until Malcolm Canmore (or "Bigmouth") managed to have Lulach killed as well. Lulach is both in the play and not in it: he is in it as the babe to whom Lady Macbeth had

Duncan fervently exclaims, "O valiant cousin, worthy gentleman".

Unlike the bleeding Captain, who is so badly wounded he collapses before he can finish his speech, Duncan has no real sense of the horrors of prolonged, savage combat in a climate so cold that swords *smoke* when they are pulled from *reeking* wounds. Indeed when the Captain does collapse from his wounds, Duncan's response is similarly disengaged. He tells the captain his wounds are *becoming*:

"given suck", but he is not in it in that we never see or hear anything more about him. Lulach is a no less obscure figure in the *Oxford Illustrated History of the British Monarchy*: he is not listed in the index, although his brief reign is recorded in the book's unnumbered yellow pages.

Kenneth Muir's claim that Shakespeare "suppresses the facts" in Holinshed sounds more historical than it is; it follows from Muir's interpretative view that Shakespeare made his Duncan old and saintly and "blackened" Macbeth's character, but this interpretative reading can be questioned, just as my own dissenting interpretative reading can be questioned. H.N. Paul's thesis that Shakespeare wrote his play to please the incoming Scottish monarch also sounds more historical than it is, and depends on an extreme and implausible interpretation of the play. There is no historical or documentary support whatsoever for the claim – which is still repeated by contemporary and very influential American critics like Stephen Orgel – that there was a special court peformance of *Macbeth*.◆

So well thy words become thee as thy wounds,
They smack of honour both.

But if at first Duncan seems old and feeble, he soon shows himself to be cunning and, in his own way, formidable. Once he is sure that Macbeth and Banquo have saved Scotland and his own royal skin, he becomes very purposeful in pressing a carefully prepared agenda, the main item of which is to establish his elder son Malcolm as Prince of Cumberland and heir to the throne. To accomplish this, he must first assemble all the thanes or Scottish lords whose traditional powers he wants to curtail or deny – with their consent.

Why? Because, according to the Scottish rules of 'tanistry', or succession, it was the thanes' historic right to *elect* the new King from within the extended royal family. In the *Chronicles*, it is clear that the historical Makbeth's chief motive for killing Duncan had nothing to do with the Weird Sisters, but followed directly from Makbeth's being so "sorely troubled" by the historical Duncan's attempt to "defraud" him – note that strong word! – of his own claim to the throne.

Just how strong that claim is remains a murky point in the play, yet it is clear that in Shakespeare's version of the story, as in Holinshed's, Macbeth has *some* claim, which he has talked about with his wife before he meets the

Weird Sisters, and clear that the Scottish rules of succession did not depend on primogeniture: some kind of election was involved, in the Scotland of *Macbeth* as in the Denmark of *Hamlet*. What Duncan is about to do – and to do to his first cousin Macbeth, whom he correctly calls his "worthiest cousin" – is not only wrong but, as Arthur Kinney puts it in *Lies Like Truth*, an "act of tyranny".

Duncan, who is aware of this, seeks to appease Macbeth. He dispatches Angus and Ross to find his worthiest cousin and Banquo. Angus tells Macbeth he has come

> *To give thee from our royal master thanks,*
> *Only to herald thee into his sight,*
> *Not pay thee. [1.3]*

This hint of some prospective payment is naturally exciting, and to make the saviour of Scotland its next King, or Prince of Cumberland, would make sense. All the more so, from Macbeth's point of view, when Ross delivers the still more exciting other part of the King's message:

> *And for an earnest of a greater honour*
> *He bade me, from him, call thee Thane of*
> *Cawdor.*

To become the new Thane of Cawdor is a great

"honour", but Macbeth is far more excited by this promise, or "earnest", of a still "greater honour". When Laurence Olivier played Macbeth at Stratford, he had his Macbeth suppose that *he* was to be declared heir to the throne – or Prince of Cumberland. As he told Kenneth Tynan, in the fourth scene a prince's coronet was lying on a pillow beside Duncan: "I looked at it, and sort of registered, 'Oh, already, fine." This was one possible answer to the question of what the "greater honour" might be.

But what Macbeth could not know or guess was that there was to be no "greater honour" of any kind: Duncan's promise turns out to be empty – no more than a means of ensuring that Macbeth and the other generals and thanes are present to hear, and endorse, what he has planned for the "boy Malcolm":

> *Sons, kinsmen, thanes,*
> *And you whose places are the nearest, know*
> *We will establish our estate upon*
> *Our eldest, Malcolm, whom we name hereafter*
> *The Prince of Cumberland. [1.4]*

This, as we have seen, comes as a complete shock to Macbeth. And many critics, among them critics who subscribed to the traditional providentialist view of Duncan as a saintly king, from A.C. Bradley down, have also been startled by the astonishing "abruptness" of his investiture of Malcolm as his successor. Many thought some bit of the play must be missing. Yet that shock isn't so surprising, especially if we have read the relevant stretches of the *Chronicles* about the feeble but crafty Duncan. As Bob Dylan has so often exclaimed in interviews or before difficult audiences, "Come on! Give me a break!"

Further evidence that Shakespeare drew heavily on Holinshed in his portrayal of Duncan comes in the way the people around the supposedly "Holy King" behave towards him. In fact the most sensitive registering of Duncan's "virtues" comes paradoxically, from his murderer – Macbeth himself. Nobody else speaks about Duncan as warmly as he does. Indeed it is when he begins to think of Duncan in his first soliloquy that the floodgates open: both his real but suppressed revulsion at the deed he contemplates, and the "milk of human kindness" that his wife fears, erupt, overwhelming his attempt to weigh his options in a cool, prudential way:

> *Besides, this Duncan*
> *Has borne his faculties so meek, hath been*
> *So clear in his great office, that his virtues*
> *Will plead like angels, trumpet-tongued against*
> *The deep damnation of his taking off... [1.7]*

To Lady Macbeth, he is just the "old man" who

stands in their way, although she is unnerved when the sleeping Duncan reminds her of her father. Macduff's horror when he discovers the murdered Duncan tells us nothing at all about Duncan's personal qualities; his reaction to the death is a religious one; he calls it this "most sacrilegious murder".

Nor do Duncan's sons ever speak to or about him with anything like personal affection. Malcolm's famous response when he is told "Your royal father's murdered", is to ask, "O, by whom?" An actor's nightmare: suppose somebody laughs. When the young Paul Scofield played Malcolm he astounded the audience by shouting the question; other actors have tried to fill out the question by suggesting that Malcolm's first response is completely stunned. Well maybe, but Malcolm's next response is to whisper urgently with his brother Donalbain about what they need to do to ensure their personal safety, regardless of what then happens to the country they abandon. In the later, so-called "English" scene, Malcolm has opportunity enough to speak of his father's virtues, but never does; the King he praises for being good and even holy is not his dead father but the English King Edward I. As Harry T. Berger observes:

A striking fact about the play is that hardly anybody speaks at all about Duncan after he is dead. With the exception of the Macbeths, no one speaks of him as a human being, a loved and loving father, a man as well as a king, who should be an object of pity as well as reverence or terror. They speak of him in terms of kingship or terror only – as a thing, a symbol, the source of their former good and present fear. They evince great respect but little fellow feeling, great horror but little pity.

We should also notice that the Scottish lords, or thanes, pay no heed to Duncan's wishes that his elder son, Malcolm, should succeed him. Not one thane, not even Macduff, falls to his knees when Malcolm appears and is told of his father's death. Instead they ignore Malcolm's investiture as the new Prince of Cumberland and immediately reassume their old right to elect the new King: Macbeth's election is unopposed, and in the play he sets off on the very same day to be crowned and anointed at Scone. Nor is there is any suggestion that Macbeth has promised the other thanes rewards for choosing him, as Duncan promised them rewards for accepting Malcolm as Prince of Cumberland, or as Malcolm himself promises rewards when he becomes king in the final scene. Macbeth is chosen because his fellow thanes want him to be king. Malcolm is too frightened for his safety to assert his doubtful right to the throne, or care what happens to his country, while Macduff is quite wrong when he later describes Macbeth as a "usurper". He is not a usurper. He is properly elected and "anointed" as Scotland's rightful king.

In Shakespeare's play Macbeth sneers at the "English epicures", and the historical Macbeth was a true Scot – fiercely opposed to the Duncan-Malcolm cultivation of the "English", who obligingly send a ten-thousand strong army to assist the small Scottish contingent and buttress Malcolm's doubtful claim.

All of these matters deserve more attention than they have usually received, and should give us pause before accepting the traditional view of Duncan as "the Holy King". They cast doubt on Kenneth Muir's confidently traditional assertion that Shakespeare simply ignored Holinshed's assessment of Duncan. On the contrary, the textual evidence of Macbeth suggests that Shakespeare and Holinshed saw Duncan in much the same way.

How good a man is Banquo?

If critics have consistently sentimentalised Duncan they have done much the same with Banquo, Macbeth's friend and the general who fights alongside him and is with him when the witches make their prophecies. The conventional view is that Banquo is a good if limited man who resists temptation.

He is certainly limited. "*Unpossessedness*", the inspired word that Coleridge chose to describe Banquo's mind, is wonderfully felicitous: it suggests something attractive but simple-minded, and not "possessed" by any imaginative terrors:

> O how truly Shakespearean is the opening of Macbeth's character given in the *unpossessedness* of Banquo's mind, wholly present to the present object – an unsullied, unscarified mirror...

A little later in his "Marginalia on 'Macbeth'", Coleridge drew a further contrast between Macbeth's undeniably *possessed* mind – or much richer imagination – and that of Banquo, when they have heard the prophecies that concern Macbeth's future and Banquo asks the Weird Sisters about his own:

> The questions of Banquo [are] those of natural curiosity – such as a girl would make after she had heard a gypsy tell her schoolfellow's fortune – all perfectly general, or rather *planless*. But Macbeth, lost in thought, raises himself to speech only by their being about to depart: '*Stay*, you imperfect speakers'; and all that follows is reasoning on a problem already discussed in his mind – on a hope which he welcomes, and the

doubts concerning its attainment he wishes to have cleared up. His eagerness, the eager eye with which he had pursued their evanition, compared with the easily satisfied mind of the self-uninterested Banquo...

"Would they had stayed!", Macbeth exclaims. But Banquo's "wonder" at their departure is, as Coleridge remarks, "that of any spectator": "Were such things here?"

Macbeth is "temptable" because he has already thought about becoming King. What Coleridge calls the "germ" was already there. When he hears the third Sister say that he will be "King hereafter" Macbeth doesn't say anything, but "starts" with a shock that Banquo immediately notices:

Good sir, why do you start, and seem to fear
Things that sound so fair? [1.3]

In *Shakespeare the Thinker* (2007), A.D. Nuttall describes this "start" as the "most economical feat of dramaturgy ever, the place where most is done in least time" – that is, in "less than a second":

What does the start mean? Some say that it simply signifies surprise. Others more shrewdly say, "No, it means recognition." If he had merely been surprised, Macbeth would have said, in Jacobean English, "Why on

TEN FACTS
ABOUT *MACBETH*

1.

Macbeth is both Shakespeare's last tragedy, and the shortest – at about 2,100 lines it is not much more than half as long as *Hamlet* , which has 3,924.

2.

Macbeth speaks more than 30 per cent of the lines of the play (Lady Macbeth speaks 11 per cent) - a dominance unmatched in any other play by Shakespeare.

3.

It is believed by some that Shakespeare – who often took bit parts in his plays – would have played the part of King Duncan.

4.

Macbeth is probably the most performed play ever written; it has been said that a performance is staged somewhere in the world every four hours.

5.

Some people believe that contemporary practitioners of black magic were so dismayed by the play's detailed exposure of witchcraft that they cursed the play. And it certainly has a history of misfortune and calamity. Some of the more unlucky productions include: the 1942 production with John Gielgud in the lead role, in which three actors died and the costume and set designer killed himself on the set; the 1849 production in New York Place, when a riot broke out and 31 people were trampled to death; and the 1971 production starting David Leary, blighted by two fires and seven robberies.

6.

Whether the Macbeths have any children has been the subject of much heated debate – so much so that it often obscures the play's more interesting aspects. In 1933 the critic L.C. Knights put an end to the debate with his essay, "How Many Children Had Lady Macbeth?" in which he argued that speculation about fictional characters' lives outside of what the fiction tells us is futile.

Roman Polanski and Jon Finch on the set of the 1971 film

7.

Macbeth has been adapted for the screen countless times – perhaps the most famous film adaptations are Roman Polansnki's 1971 film and the Korean director Akira Kirosawa's 1957 classic, *Throne of Blood*. It has also inspired two major operas – one by Giuseppe Verdi and one by Ernest Bloch. It has been turned into cartoons, graphic novels, and forms the basis of many plays – most recently Punchdrunk's promenade production, *Sleep No More*, in which the plot of *Macbeth* was intertwined with the plot of Daphne du Maurier's *Rebecca*.

8.

The most frequently occurring words in the play are "blood" and "night", each of which occurs – in various forms – more than 40 times.

uMabatha, *the South African playwright Welcome Msomi's adaptation of* Macbeth, *set in an early 19th-century Zulu tribe, The Globe, 2003*

9.

Except for the appearance of the ghost of Hamlet's father, the only other play in Shakespeare's canon to feature the supernatural is *Julius Caesar*, which had shortly preceded *Macbeth*. The two plays are in many ways quite similar.

10.

It is not known how much of *Macbeth* Shakespeare actually wrote, though it is generally accepted that there are parts of it he didn't. Act three, Scene five and Act four, Scene one are thought to have been written by Thomas Middleton, author of *The Changeling* and *Women Beware Women*. These scenes are usually cut from modern productions. Middleton is also thought to be responsible for a number of lines in *Measure for Measure* – possibly as much as 10 per cent of the play.

earth do you say *that*?" The companion, Banquo, is himself puzzled, as he would never have been by simple amazement, and detects a note of fear. Macbeth's start means, "How do they know that I have already thought about that happening?"

But while Macbeth is tempted, because he has already thought about becoming King, Banquo is not. How could he be? As Coleridge's beautifully judged account of the "unpossessed", "self-uninterested" Banquo suggests, he simply accepts

THE WEIRD SISTERS

When she is called a "witch" by the rash woman who wouldn't share her chestnuts, the first of the Weird Sisters is roused to such a vengeful fury that she determines to plague the woman's husband, who has sailed "to Aleppo" as "master of the Tiger":

in a sieve I'll thither sail,

And like rat without a tail,
I'll do, I'll do, and I'll do.

Rats are notoriously active, sexually, and a rat without a tail would be constantly available. This, and the First Sister's determination to "drain" the man, suggests that she will torment him sexually as a succubus, while also ensuring that The Tiger is "tempest-tossed":

I'll drain him dry as hay;
Sleep shall neither night nor day
Hang upon his penthous lid;
He shall live a man forbid.
Weary sev'n nights, nine times nine,

what the witches say. Besides, there isn't as yet any temptation he needs to resist. He has been told that he will beget a line of kings. There is nothing he can do to help that happen, other than looking after Fleance and maybe having more children.

So when Macbeth and Banquo discuss their encounter with the Weird Sisters in the third scene, Macbeth asks Banquo,

> *Do you not hope your children shall be kings,*
> *When those that gave the Thane of Cawdor*
> *to me,*

Shall he dwindle, peak, and pine.

Macbeth and Banquo never hear the Weird Sisters talk like this. As the great German critic A.W. Schlegel noted, as soon as Macbeth and Banquo enter the witches immediately "assume a loftier tone": their "predictions" then "have all the obscure brevity, the majestic solemnity of oracles, such as have ever spread terror among mortals".

Sailing in a sieve or bottomless boat, killing swine, engaging in unimaginable sexual activities that we like trying to imagine, causing tempests, flying into frenzies of menace when accused of being a witch: these things were all standard items in the lore of witchcraft. As soon as they heard the Weird Sisters talk like this in the third scene, many spectators in the first audiences would have concluded at once that the Weird Sisters are witches. On the other hand, this malicious bugaboo chatter is what made Bradley so sure that these old women – "poor and ragged, skinny and hideous, full of vulgar spirit"–are not, "in any way whatever, supernatural beings".◆

Promised no less to them?

In his sunnily open, or (to recall Coleridge again) still "unsullied" and "unscarified" way, Banquo replies:

> *That trusted home*
> *Might yet enkindle you unto the crown,*
> *Besides the Thane of Cawdor. But 'tis strange;*
> *And oftentimes, to win us to our harm,*
> *The instruments of darkness tell us truths,*
> *Win us with honest trifles, to betray's*
> *In deepest consequence.*

His warning to Macbeth is morally sensible or prudent, and very much to the point. (Horatio

---

INVENTING BANQUO

Like Shakespeare's Macduff, Banquo was not "born of woman" – though for a quite different reason. Banquo was "born" in Paris in 1527, when Hector Boece (or "Boethius") published his *Scotorum Historiae* or history of the Scottish people and obligingly presented his royal Scottish patron James V with a mythological ancestor and a lineage going back half a millenium. As Boece explained, Banquo was "the beginner of the Stewarts in this realm, from whom our King now present by long and ancient lineage is descended". But Banquo never existed. He was Boece's invention.

The King was naturally delighted by this account of his own awesomely long lineage. According to a tradition that may or may should have said something like this to Hamlet.) But it is not morally profound. It hasn't yet dawned on Banquo that his – and Fleance's – situation will be much more dangerous if Macbeth does become King. Once that shadow falls, Banquo will become "temptable", and more and more frightened. (This development, incidentally, is all Shakespeare's invention, since he has made his Banquo quite unlike the Banquo of the *Chronicles*, who was Macbeth's accomplice in Duncan's murder.) The scene ends with Macbeth saying to Banquo, as they set off to meet Duncan,

> *Think upon what hath chanced, and at more time.*

not be reliable, he could not even read Latin; but he immediately commissioned two translations into Scots, one into prose and the other in verse. Doubtless, he wanted to read Boece's wonderful work for himself, but he would have been even more concerned that others should read it. John Bellenden's prose translation, *Croniklis of the Scots*, appeared first in 1536, and was most widely read – not least by Holinshed and Francis Thynne, the Scottish expert in Holinshed's team who was almost entirely responsible for the Scottish part of the *Chronicles*. They would both have been astonished to learn that Banquo was a mythical invention. So would Shakespeare, who could not read labour-saving books with titles like *Shakespeare's Holinshed*, and had plodded through the 60-odd pages that "show", in an entirely fictitious way, how the "Steward", "Stewart" or Stuart kings all

The interim having weighed it, let us speak
Our free hearts each to other.

Banquo, whose heart is still "free" and whose imagination is not being consumed, like Macbeth's, by some "horrid image", replies in his still guileless way: "Very gladly".

But, significantly, Banquo decides not to mention the encounter with the Weird Sisters to anybody, before or after Duncan's murder. As Harry Berger observed in his brilliantly unsettling 1980 essay on "The Early Scenes of *Macbeth*", when Banquo is talking with his King as they enter Macbeth's castle in the sixth scene he does not mention the Weird Sisters, talking instead about

descended from Banquo, who never existed.

The first history of the Scottish people was John of Fordun's ambitious and impressively researched *Chronica Gentis Scotorum* (1363). This was also the first historical account in which Macduff, "the excellent, noble and loyal thane of Fife", emerged as Malcolm's principal supporter. However, the murder of Macduff's family was another Boece invention.

As Ian Aitchison observes in his admirable and lively *Macbeth: Man and Myth* (1999), Fordun's eloquent account of the "tyrannous" Macbeth's "oppression" was "uncorroborated by contemporary sources". Like Boece's early 16th-century account, Fordun's late 14th-century account was prompted by the wish or need to emphasise "the continuity of Scottish kingship to counter English claims of historical overlordship".◆

"temple-haunting martlets".

Yet by the beginning of Act Two he has become both "temptable" and terrified, when he beseeches the "merciful powers" to "restrain in me the cursed thoughts that nature/Gives way to in repose".

Then, when Macbeth enters, Banquo confides to him that he "dreamed last night of the three Weird Sisters". Macbeth agrees to talk about this at a moment when they both have time, but assures Banquo that

If you shall cleave to my consent, when 'tis,
It shall make honour for you. [2.1]

This is a promise, but in return for what? The guarded, frightened Banquo replies, "So [long as] I lose none/ In seeking to augment it."

But that stops short of saying that he will not support Macbeth if he kills Duncan. After the murder, he expresses his determination to fight against "treasonous malice" while avoiding even the slightest hint that he suspects foul play by Macbeth. That is his public voice, however. In his soliloquy at the beginning of Act Three, we hear what he privately fears – and the word "yet" both explains and conceals from himself the reason why he has just approved Macbeth's election as King:

Thou hast it now, King, Cawdor, Glamis, all,
As the Weird Women promised, and I fear

As the Weird Women promised, and I fear
Thou playd'st most foully for't; yet it was said
It should not stand in thy posterity,
But that myself should be the root and father
Of many kings. [3.1]

In short, Banquo equivocates, and goes on
equivocating until his dreadful death. He is tested,
and he fails the test. Here again, as with Duncan,
the providentialist readings flatten out a complex
and interesting character and fail to do justice to the
subtlety of Shakespeare's art.

Francesca Annis and Jon Finch in Roman Polanski's film of Macbeth, *(1971)*

Opposite: photograph of the first page of Macbeth *from a facsimile
edition of the First Folio of Shakespeare's plays, published in 1623*

THE TRAGEDIE OF
MACBETH.

Actus Primus. Scœna Prima.

Thunder and Lightning. Enter three Witches.

1. **H**En shall we three meet againe?
In Thunder, Lightning, or in Raine?
2. When the Hurley-burley's done,
When the Battaile's lost, and wonne.
3. That will be ere the set of Sunne.
1. Where the place?
2. Vpon the Heath.
3. There to meet with *Macbeth*.
1. I come, *Gray-Malkin*.
All. *Padock* calls anon: faire is foule, and foule is faire,
Houer through the fogge and filthie ayre. *Exeunt.*

Scena Secunda.

Alarum within. Enter King Malcolme, Donalbaine, Lenox, with attendants, meeting a bleeding Captaine.

King. What bloody man is that? he can report,
As seemeth by his plight, of the Reuolt
The newest state.

Mal. This is the Serieant,
Who like a good and hardie Souldier fought
'Gainst my Captiuitie : Haile braue friend ;
Say to the King, the knowledge of the Broyle,
As thou didst leaue it.

Cap. Doubtfull it stood,
As two spent Swimmers, that doe cling together,
And choake their Art : The mercilesse *Macdonwald*
(Worthie to be a Rebell, for to that
The multiplying Villanies of Nature
Doe swarme vpon him) from the Westerne Isles
Of Kernes and Gallowgrosses is supply'd,
And Fortune on his damned Quarry smiling,
Shew'd like a Rebells Whore : but all's too weake :
For braue *Macbeth* (well hee deserues that Name)
Disdayning Fortune, with his brandisht Steele,
Which smoak'd with bloody execution
(Like Valours Minion) caru'd out his passage,
Till hee fac'd the Slaue :
Which neu'r shooke hands, nor bad farewell to him,
Till he vnseam'd him from the Naue toth' Chops,
And fix'd his Head vpon our Battlements.

King. O valiant Cousin, worthy Gentleman.

Cap. As whence the Sunne 'gins his reflection,
Shipwracking Stormes, and direfull Thunders :
So from that Spring, whence comfort seem'd to come,
Discomfort swells : Marke King of Scotland, marke,
No sooner Iustice had, with Valour arm'd,
Compell'd these skipping Kernes to trust their heeles,
But the Norweyan Lord, surueying vantage,
With furbusht Armes, and new supplyes of men,
Began a fresh assault.

King. Dismay'd not this our Captaines, *Macbeth* a*n*
Banquoh?

Cap. Yes, as Sparrowes, Eagles ;
Or the Hare, the Lyon :
If I say sooth, I must report they were
As Cannons ouer-charg'd with double Cracks,
So they doubly redoubled stroakes vpon the Foe :
Except they meant to bathe in reeking Wounds,
Or memorize another *Golgotha*,
I cannot tell : but I am faint,
My Gashes cry for helpe.

King. So well thy words become thee, as thy woun*ds*
They smack of Honor both : Goe get him Surgeons.

Enter Rosse and Angus.

Who comes here ?

Mal. The worthy Thane of *Rosse*.

Lenox. What a haste lookes through his eyes ?
So should he looke, that seemes to speake things stra*ng*

Rosse. God saue the King.

King. Whence cam'st thou, worthy *Thane* ?

Rosse. From Fiffe, great King,
Where the Norweyan Banners flowt the Skie,
And fanne our people cold.
Norway himselfe, with terrible numbers,
Assisted by that most disloyall Traytor,
The *Thane* of Cawdor, began a dismall Conflict,
Till that *Bellona's* Bridegroome, lapt in proofe,
Confronted him with selfe-comparisons,
Point against Point, rebellious Arme 'gainst Arme,
Curbing his lauish spirit : and to conclude,
The Victorie fell on vs.

King. Great happinesse.

Rosse. That now *Sweno*, the Norwayes King,
Craues composition :
Nor would we deigne him buriall of his men,
Till he disbursed, at Saint *Colmes* ynch,
Ten thousand Dollars, to our generall vse.

How close is the Macbeths' marriage?

Shakespeare doesn't do happy marriages, but *Macbeth* includes his most extended exploration of a marriage between two people who love each other deeply and have lived together for a long time.

In his other plays, the nearest competition comes in *Julius Caesar*: Brutus and Portia also love each other deeply, although their marriage, like Macbeth's, is torn apart by politics – or by what Shakespeare so frequently presents as the conflict between love values and power values. Portia speaks movingly of what marriage means, or should mean, when she is asking her husband why she is in the "suburbs" of his pleasure:

> *Within the bond of marriage, tell me, Brutus,*
> *Is it excepted I should know no secrets*
> *That appertain to you? Am I your self*
> *But, as it were, in sort or limitation,*
> *To keep with you at meals, comfort your bed,*
> *And talk to you sometimes? Dwell I but in the*
>   *suburbs*
> *Of your good pleasure? If it be no more,*
> *Portia is Brutus' harlot, not his wife.*

Romeo and Juliet can't count as competitors; although they are passionately in love and marry, they have no time to live together. The same is true of Othello and Desdemona: they are allowed no more private time together, as man and wife, than Romeo and Juliet.

The middle-aged lovers in *Antony and Cleopatra,* the play that followed *Macbeth,* can't count as competitors either, but for a more complicated and interesting reason. They are married — but not to each other; Antony's loveless marriage to Octavius Caesar's sister Octavia is dictated by political expediencies. Significantly, Cleopatra has children by Antony as well as by Julius Caesar; but Antony never shows interest in his children, and Cleopatra is a "deadbeat mum", as John Sutherland argues in an amusing but pointed essay.

Antony and Cleopatra is Shakespeare's most sustained exploration of Grand Passion – not married love. So, in the first scene we hear Antony proclaim:

> *Let Rome in Tiber melt, and the wide arch*
> *Of the rang'd empire fall! Here is my space,*
> *Kingdoms are clay; our dungy earth alike*
> *Feeds beast as man; the nobleness of life*
> *Is to do thus –*

before he embraces or kisses Cleopatra in public. The Macbeths never talk or behave like this, even in private. Nor do the Macduffs, in the play's other marriage. Indeed, Macduff could be regarded as Antony's opposite: Antony soon abandons his loveless marriage and Roman values to be with Cleopatra again, whereas Macduff abandons his wife and children to serve his King and Country.

Coleridge saw no sign of "domestic" tenderness between the Macbeths, and coldly noted how, when Macbeth finally returns home after saving his King and Country, Lady Macbeth shows "No womanly, no wifely joy at the return of her husband; no retrospection on the dangers he had escaped."

This, however ignores something that seems decidedly and movingly marital in the habitual way these lovers take each other for granted, which is a blessing as well as a danger in any marriage, and altogether distinguishes their mutual love from Grand Passion of the *Antony and Cleopatra* variety. Macbeth's own first words, when he enters in Act One, Scene Six, are "My dearest love", but these words are not a romantic declaration. They are an almost automatic or unthinking but not unfelt address, before the pressingly urgent information that "Duncan comes here tonight". Lady Macbeth just *is* his "dearest love", and they both know that. She doesn't respond with some similarly casual but similarly loving endearment, although they are probably embracing each other at this point. They talk about their immediate concern, like a married couple who haven't seen each other for a time but plunge straight into a discussion of, say, their son's university fees. Later, when Macbeth says "O, full of scorpions is my mind, dear wife", the unthinking casualness of "dear wife" reveals the corner of his mind that is still not full of scorpions. A few lines later, he calls her "dearest chuck".

Within this long established, habitual but loving relationship, Lady Macbeth behaves as she thinks a traditional "good wife" should. She goads him terribly when she thinks he is not looking after his own as well as their interests, but hesitates to say anything which might unnerve him. When he declares "We will proceed no further in this business", she accuses him of breaking a promise that we never heard him make:

> What beast was't then
> That made you break this enterprise to me?
> When you durst do it, then you were a man;
> And to be more than what you were, you would
> Be so much more the man. Nor time and place
> Did then cohere, and yet you would make both –
> They have made themselves, and that their
> fitness now
> Does unmake you. I have given suck, and know
> How tender 'tis to love the babe that milks me;
> I would, while it was smiling in my face,
> Have pluck'd my nipple from his boneless gums
> And dash'd the brains out, had I so sworn
> As you have done to this. [1.7]

Here she is speaking as a loyal wife who knows what her husband wants to do and needs to do. She is no less loyal when she privately admits her despair in Act Three, Scene Two:

> *Nought's had, all's spent,*
> *Where our desire is got without content;*
> *'Tis safer to be that which we destroy,*
> *Than by destruction dwell in doubtful joy –*

But she would never dream of telling her husband (who enters at this point) how her own mind is full of scorpions. Because they are or have been so close, and because he does not hesitate to confide in her, he then utters the very same thought that she keeps to herself:

> *Better to be with the dead,*
> *Whom we, to gain our peace, have sent to peace,*
> *Than on the torture of the mind to lie*
> *In restless ecstasy...*

Instead of saying "Oh, my love, that's just what I was thinking!", she says "Come on"! –

> *Come on –*
> *Gentle my lord, sleek o'er your rugged looks ...*

This recalls her earlier responses when the terrified Macbeth keeps telling her how he "could not say 'Amen'". At first she says, "Consider it not so deeply", but then, when he persists in telling her yet again how the words "Stuck in my throat", she replies in a more desperately concerned and lovingly frightened way:

> These deeds must not be thought
> After these ways: so, it will make us mad. [2.2]

But, of course, it is too late. By murdering Duncan, Macbeth has already destroyed himself – and his marriage.

What happens to the marriage?

When Macbeth is left alone, before the murder, we see him plunging into the abyss, the phantom dagger overwhelming his "heat-oppressed brain". His terror at the hallucination suggests, as Wilbur Sanders says, "incipient insanity", and in the preternatural silence of the night, there is a suggestion, in the soliloquy, that "the body itself has become detached from the observing mind, a strange disembodied somnambulism in which Macbeth, as in a dream, watches himself moving 'like a Ghost', beyond possibility of control or recall".

The same "present horror" goes on in the next scene, when, after the murder, Macbeth's self-division becomes even more terrifying as he contemplates his hands as if they belonged to some stranger:

What hands are here? Ha, they pluck out mine eyes. [2.2]

Macbeth does not know his own hands: "his deed has created a reality of evil outside himself". But now that his own self is so divided he realizes there is only one solution:

THE POETRY IN *MACBETH*

When Macbeth has rejoined his wife after murdering Duncan, the First Folio version of their strained, intensely urgent exchange provides an extraordinary example of how simple and conversationally intimate Shakespeare's language and verse can be, when he wants to be "realistic":

MAC. I have done the deed:
Didst thou not heare a noyse?
LADY. I heard the Owle schreame, and the Crickets cry.
Did not you speake?
MAC. When?
LADY. Now.
MAC As I descended?
LADY. I [Ay].
MAC. Hearke, who lyes i'th' second Chamber?
LADY MAC. Donalbaine.
MAC. This is a sorry sight.
LADY MAC. A foolish thought, to say a sorry sight.

However, since this doesn't

To know my deed,
'Twere best not know my selfe.

He sees, as Sanders says, that he cannot both grasp
the true nature of what he has done *and* go on
living amicably with himself.

> If he continues to know himself (the self he has
> been) the deed is incredible and monstrous. If he
> grasps the reality of the deed he is alienated from
> himself and can no longer recognise the bloody
> hand as his own. (It is in the nature of an evil act
> to drive this wedge between deed and doer, so
> that acceptance of the deed involves

---

even look like verse, many
modern readers might not
hear that it is verse unless
they are reading a nanny-like
modern edition that spreads
the lines across the page to
show that they are indeed
verse, not prose:

MACBETH.
I have done the deed. Didst
    thou not hear a noise?
LADY MACBETH.
I heard the owl scream, and the
    crickets cry.
Did you not speak?
MACBETH.
    When?

LADY MACBETH.
    Now.
MACBETH.
        As I descended?
LADY MACBETH.
Ay.
MACBETH.
Hark – who lies i'th'second
    chamber?
LADY MACBETH.
        Donalbain.
MACBETH.
This is a sorry sight.
LADY MACBETH.
    A foolish thought,
    To say a sorry sight.

Presumably, but it's a

estrangement from the self.) Very well, he will know the deed. He will make his peace with it, build his life around it, accept it as fact. What he will not do is *own* the deed – acknowledge it as the work of the general, Macbeth, loyal vassal of the gracious Duncan. To that self he bids an anguished farewell in these lines, beginning the construction of a new 'self' whose premise is murder.

The play presents what happens to the Macbeths and their marriage through two sharply contrasted arcs. When we first see Macbeth he is the saviour of Scotland but a nervous wreck, not unlike a

humbling thought, the First Folio editors thought that its readers could hear what was verse without any need for graphic or visual aids. In the 18th century Alexander Pope was the first Shakespeare editor to print Pistol's pseudo-heroic verse in *Henry V* as verse, not prose, but the editors of the First Folio evidently assumed that the Folio's readers would hear, like the play's first spectators, that Pistol's verse was indeed verse, and a hilarious pseudo-heroic parody of the "heroic" verse in Marlowe and other contemporary dramatists. Hamlet and most Elizabethans spoke of going to hear, not see, a play. Some years later, in his Prologue to *The New Inn* (1629), Ben Jonson noticed and derided the new tendency to speak of "seeing" a play. But most contemporary Shakespeare critics write as though Shakespeare's poetic dramas were, or might as well have been, written in prose.◆

shell-shocked soldier in World War One, who can barely remember what he was fighting for. His meeting with the Weird Sisters impregnates his mind with a "horrid image" that

> *doth unfix my hair*
> *And make my seated heart knock at my ribs*
> *Against the use of nature... [1.3]*

And yet, however shocking it may seem to say so, Macbeth only recovers his strength when he determines to act. And then, after the murder, he becomes more and more determined to do whatever must be done, until, after the banquet scene in Act Three, he is talking only of what must be done "for mine own good": his wife is forgotten, the marriage is over, and we never see them together again.

Lady Macbeth moves in exactly the opposite direction. At first, in her two soliloquies in Act One, Scene Five, she seems astonishingly steely, inviting spirits to unsex and denature her, and giving vent to her fierce "fear" that her husband's "nature" is "too full o'th'milk of human kindess" – so that he is "not without ambition, but without/ The illness should attend on it".

Yet even in this first soliloquy she is lovingly loyal to her own sense of what her husband really wants and needs. In her driven, fiercely passionate view, what he wants "highly" is a real need; what he wants "holily" is no more than a fancied need. He should put "human kindness" behind him and kill the "old man" who stands in their way.

So we have those contrasting arcs, which made Freud think that Macbeth and his "Lady" (who is never called Lady Macbeth in the play) are two halves of the same disembodied person. That is far-fetched, but it is true that Macbeth starts as a nervous wreck and becomes stronger, though less human, while Lady Macbeth starts as an Iron Lady and becomes weaker, though more human. She is revealingly disturbed when the sleeping Duncan reminds her of her father, but what really destroys her is not guilt or remorse over the murder of Duncan: it is the sense of increasing estrangement within their marriage.

So, in Act Three, Scene Two, she has to tell the servant that she wants to speak to Macbeth, and then asks her husband. "How now, my lord, why do you keep alone...?" It's worth noticing how she always calls him "My lord" after he becomes King. The conversation about Banquo and Fleance that follows is odd, in a way that measures their growing estrangement. Macbeth has not told his wife that he has already arranged for Banquo and Fleance to be murdered, and now he tells his wife to pay special attention to Banquo among the guests at the banquet, although he knows Banquo will not be there. Then, as in the past, he suddenly confides in her:

O, full of scorpions is my mind, dear wife –
Thou know'st that Banquo and his Fleance
lives. [3.2]

Her response is chilling, unambiguous, and
characteristically unhesitating: "But in them
nature's copy's not eterne." What happens next
seems strange and disconcerting, above all for
her if she senses the growing estrangement. First,
Macbeth strongly hints at what he has planned:
"There's comfort yet, they are assailable", and
this night "there shall be done/ A deed of dreadful
note". But then, when she very naturally asks,
"What's to be done?" he still will not tell her:

Be innocent of the knowledge, dearest chuck,
Till thou applaud the deed. Come, seeling night,
Scarf up the tender eye of pitiful day...

"Thou marvell'st at my words, but hold thee still",
he says, before leading her off to the banquet.

In the climactic banquet scene Macbeth is the
only person onstage who sees Banquo's ghost.
Lady Macbeth is helplessly unaware of what is
happening, but all the more breathtakingly loyal
and inventive in trying to "cover" for her husband –
until she finally gives up and tells the assembled
thanes to leave at once without regard for "the
order of their going". But then, amazingly, there
is no discussion of what has happened when they

are finally alone together. Instead of being fierce or reproachful, or wanting an explanation, Lady Macbeth is desperately solicitous. She tries to persuade her husband to come to bed and try to "sleep". These are the last words she ever speaks to him. Of course she is remembering this moment in the earlier scene when she sleepwalks, saying: "To bed, to bed, to bed".

Further communication between them has become impossible, now and forever. Like Portia in *Julius Caesar*, she cannot endure the breakdown of a trust and intimacy that she had for so long learned to take for granted. But Macbeth is lost in a world of his own, intent on going to find the Weird Sisters again, and on taking whatever kind of ruthless action is required "for mine own good" – not for their good. The loving, loyal Lady Macbeth has been consigned, like Portia, to the suburbs of her husband's pleasure.

Is Macduff this play's real hero?

Macbeth is barely half the length of *Hamlet*; it is the fastest, as well as the shortest, of Shakespeare's tragedies. Its furious, precipitous pace in the first three acts doesn't let up at all. But it could not proceed at such a precipitous pace if it had a "sub-plot" or counterpointing multiple plots like *King Lear*.

What we have in *Macbeth*, instead of such multiple plots, is a tersely pointed contrast between Banquo and Macduff. Both are tested, but while Banquo is found wanting, with the price of his failure to denounce Macbeth a horrible death, Macduff, in the end, passes the test and behaves like a hero – though, as we will see, his heroism, like everything else in this play, is far from straightforward.

Until the beginning of Act Four, we see relatively little of Macduff, the Scottish nobleman who goes to wake the King and finds him murdered. Unconvinced that the murder is the work of Duncan's servants, he doesn't attend Macbeth's coronation, instead going home to Fife, and fails to attend the banquet in Act Three or even to answer the invitation to it.

The result of this failure and the suspicions it arouses in Macbeth is the slaughter of his wife and child, killings which signal Macbeth's descent into the murderous abyss. He becomes the "tyrant" who says in Act Four, Scene One that he does not care if "the treasure"

Of nature's germens tumble all together,
Even till destruction sicken.

Whereas Duncan is murdered offstage, as in a Greek tragedy, the butchering of Macduff's young son takes place before our eyes in a scene that was customarily omitted, until the late 19th century, to spare the audience. However it is staged, it is an unbearable moment and one which brings home to spectators even more than to readers the idea that Macbeth's crimes are escalating, and that this attack on Nature and the Family is even worse than killing the King.

As the loyal subject who discovered the dead Duncan in Act Two, Macduff's reponse eloquently carried the theoretical and religious idea that no murder could be more "sacrilegious" than the killing of a king. But even before he learns that his own family and household have been butchered, he thinks that Macbeth must be killed.

Nevertheless, at first Macduff, like Banquo, equivocates, seemingly reluctant to denounce a properly elected and duly "anointed" king. In the so-called "English" scene in Act Four – the only slow scene in the play – he is tested by Malcolm, Duncan's son, who pretends that he is even worse than Macbeth to see how Macduff will react. Malcolm says he is insatiably lustful, and Macduff merely replies that Scotland has "willing dames enough". Malcolm goes on to say that his "avarice" is "staunchless", and that he would pick quarrels with good, loyal men simply to get his hands on their wealth. Macduff again refuses to condemn him, saying that Scotland has wealth enough "to fill up your will". Then, pushing Macduff to the limit, Malcolm insists

THE "SWEET MILK OF CONCORD"

Stephen Greenblatt once explained that pouring the "sweet milk of concord" into hell was a reference to onanism, but semen is not usually sweet or easy to pour. It is far more likely that the "sweet milk" is colostrum, which Elizabethans called "green milk" – the astonishingly sweet milk that first comes into the mother's breasts, and convinces the infant that it was worth being born. For many people (and artists) the image of a mother suckling her babe is our most deeply rooted image of "concord", and "kindness" in its older, richer sense, which was more closely linked to "kin" and "kindred". Here, of course, the reference to "milk" looks back to Lady Macbeth's "I have given suck", and her fear that her husband is "too full of th'milk of human kindness" – and to Goneril's sneering reference in *King Lear* to her own husband's "milky kindness". ◆

that he has "none" of the "king-becoming graces":

> *Nay, had I power, I should*
> *Pour the sweet milk of concord into Hell,*
> *Uproar the universal peace, confound*
> *All unity on earth.* (see p.91)

This is too much. Finally, Macduff breaks out "O Scotland, Scotland!", realising that having abandoned his family to serve king and country, he must now choose between king and country. When Malcolm says, "If such a one be fit to govern, speak", Macduff – at last, unlike Banquo, and to our immense relief – stops equivocating:

> *Fit to govern?*
> *No, not to live. O nation miserable!*

That altogether rejects the official state doctrine. It is the most politically explosive moment in the Complete Works, even more explosive than the deposition scene in *Richard II*, which was omitted (or censored) in all four quarto editions of that immensely, dangerously fascinating play. A private subject is passing judgment on a "rightful" king, in the same way that Judge John Bradshaw would sentence King Charles I to death in 1649 as a "tyrant" and "traitor" to his country. After this astonishing moment Macbeth is scarcely ever named; he becomes the "tyrant", a word which echoes through the rest of the play. He is to be killed not because he murdered Duncan (that is something Malcolm and Macduff may suspect but cannot know), and not because he is a "usurper" or "untitled" (he was properly elected and anointed at Scone), but because he is a "tyrant". Before and after *Macbeth*, the debate about whether it was ever right to kill a king who was a "tyrant" raged throughout Europe. If King James I ever saw *Macbeth* he would have been appalled by the way it comes down so strongly on the wrong side of that debate.*

But if Macduff finally emerges as the hero he pays a terrible price. The play's fourth act shows us a subtle contrast not just between Macduff and Banquo but between Macduff and Macbeth – and between their marriages. For Macbeth in the first half of the play, his "deare Wife" and "dear partner in greatness" takes precedence over all other allegiances, whereas Macduff leaves his wife and children in danger to go to England to find Malcolm. Lady Macduff's angry and deeply hurt

* The 12th chapter of David Bevington's excellent study *Tudor Drama and Politics* (1968) is devoted to "The Question of Obedience to a Tyrant". The official Tudor and Stuart line on this was very clear, as Bevington observes: "Only God could dispose of an evil yet legitimately established monarch. Since God might choose to inflict an evil ruler on a wayward people for their punishment, rebellion against His scourge would only increase divine wrath." In the trial of the Gunpowder plotters Sir Edward Coke argued that even disloyal thoughts were not permitted: "It is treason to imagine or intend the death of the King, Queen, or Prince."

wife then repeatedly calls her husband a "Traitor" for doing so. On the one hand, then, we have a "Traitor" who disregards the "Knots of Love" and "precious motives" (his wife and children), but eventually becomes a hero, while on the other we have a hero, the saviour of Scotland, whose love for his "dearest chuck" helps to make him a traitor and tyrant.

The contrast between the play's two "Ladies" is as pointed as it is unexpected. Lady Macduff seems more modern, or more like a modern single or abandoned mother. In Act Four, Scene Two, she cannot stop complaining about Macduff's abandoning her, first to her son and then to her kinsman, in front of Young Macduff. One of the most remarkable psychological aspects of this wonderful scene is the way in which her son then responds by trying to play the man, or stand in for his absent father – and is slaughted when he challenges the view that his father is a "traitor".

Another, much darker irony is that after hearing the unnamed Messenger's terribly explicit warning – "Be not found here: hence with your little ones" – Lady Macduff still cannot stop talking for long enough to try to save herself and her helpless children. But the darkest irony of all is that the scene gives further twists to this play's frightening concern with the nature of "Nature".

Opposite: Dame Ellen Terry as Lady Macbeth, 1888

The core of Lady Macduff's charge against her husband is that "He wants the natural touch": it is not "natural" to abandon your family, even to serve your King and Country. In the next scene Malcolm cannot trust Macduff for the same reason:

Perchance even there where I did find my doubts.
Why in that rawness left you wife, and child,
Those precious motives, those strong knots of love,
Without leave-taking? [4.3]

The same doubt has troubled many of the play's critics, notably W.H. Auden.* But what is most important is the way in which Lady Macduff's description of what it is to be "natural" buttresses the contrast the play forces us to make between two very different Natures – or between the world of Day and the terrifying world of Night, with its "multiplying villaines of nature". Lady Macduff protests, in her uncomprehending anguish, that

He loves us not,
He wants the natural touch. For the poor wren,
The most diminutive of birds, will fight,
Her young ones in her nest, against the owl. [4.2]

---

* It didn't trouble Verdi, who was writing his opera of *Macbeth* at a time when brave men had to leave their families to fight for Italy's future.

But of course the owl and the eagle, or the Macbeths in their marital eyrie, are no less part of Nature.

Yet another contrast that Act Four brings into sharp focus involves the play's concern with manliness. The question of what it is to be "manly" runs through the whole play, just as the question of what it is to be "womanly" runs through Shakespeare's first historical tetralogy. The most important early touchstone of this is Macbeth's unanswerable reply to his wife when she accuses him of being unmanly:

> *I dare do all that may become a man,*
> *Who dares do more is none. [1.7]*

It is a noble statement: Dr Johnson thought these two lines would have secured Shakespeare's immortality if he had written nothing else. They remind us how potentially fine Macbeth was, before he succumbed to temptation.

Macduff, in the English scene, expresses a similar sentiment, after the terrible murder of his family. His response to Ross's news is heartbreaking. For a while he cannot even take it in, and keeps asking questions like "My children too?" and "My wife too?" and "All my pretty ones? Did you say all?" He finally takes it in, and there is perhaps nothing more piercingly painful in this play than his repetition of the word "were",

MACBETH'S "BORROW'D ROBES"

A series of clothing and masking images run through
Macbeth (see opposite). As Cleanth Brooks has pointed
out, these metaphors make two key points: first, that the
garments Macbeth wants to wear, and ends up wearing,
are not his; they are stolen. "Macbeth is uncomfortable in
them because he is continually conscious of the fact that
they do not belong to him." Secondly, the oldest symbol of
the hypocrite is that of the man who cloaks his true nature
under a disguise. "Macbeth loathes the part of the
hypocrite – and actually does not play it too well."

This second point is well illustrated by a clothing image
which has sometimes been called strained. It is
Macbeth's description of the discovery of the murder in
Act Two:

> *Here lay Duncan,*
> *His silver skin lac'd with his golden blood;*
> *And his gash'd stabs look'd like a breach in nature*
> *For ruin's wasteful entrance: there, the murderers,*
> *Steep'd in the colours of their trade, their daggers*
> *Unmannerly breech'd with gore...*

Both Duncan's body and the daggers, this passage
suggests, are dressed in royal blood. And the metaphor is
in fact very apt. "As Macbeth and Lennox burst into the
room," writes Brooks, "they find the daggers wearing, as
Macbeth knows all too well, a horrible masquerade. They
have been carefully 'clothed' to play a part."

The Thane of Cawdor lives: why do you dress me
In borrow'd robes?   *(Macbeth, Act 1)*

New honours come upon him,
Like our strange garments, cleave not to their mould,
But with the aid of use.   *(Banquo, Act 1)*

He hath honour'd me of late; and I have bought
Golden opinions from all sorts of people,
Which would be worn now in their newest gloss,
Not cast aside so soon.   *(Macbeth, Act 1)*

Was the hope drunk,
Wherein you dress'd yourself?   *(Lady Macbeth, Act 1)*

Come, thick night,
And pall thee in the dunnest smoke of hell,
That my keen knife sees not the wound it makes,
Nor heaven peep through the blanket of the dark,
To cry, 'Hold, Hold!'!   *(Lady Macbeth, Act 1)*

False face must hide what the false heart doth know
                    (Macbeth to his wife, Act 2)

Scarf up the eye of pitiful day
                    (Macbeth before Banquo's murder, Act 3)

He cannot buckle his distemper'd cause
Within the belt of rule   *(Caithness, Act 5)*

---

now does he feel his title
Hang loose upon him, like a giant's robe
Upon a dwarfish thief.   *(Angus, Act 5)*

when he responds to Malcolm's callow advice to
"Dispute it like a man":

> *I shall do so:*
> *But I must also feel it as a man;*
> *I cannot but remember such things were*
> *That were most precious to me... [4.3]*

Macduff's reply to Malcolm's exhortation to be
"like a man" is devastating to the boy who would
be King: "I must also feel it as a man." We have
seen how little feeling Malcolm showed for his
murdered father, or for the fate of the country
he so hastily abandons. Even in the final scene,
Malcolm only enters Macbeth's castle when the
fighting is over, and his final speech includes
no reference to the sufferings of his country
and countrymen. Malcolm is not manly. As for
Macbeth, the inhuman depths to which he has
sunk are clear from his cauterized responses to the
death of his "dear partner in greatness":

> *She should have dy'de hereafter;*
> *There would have been time for such a word...*
> *[5.5]*

He can no longer "feel it as a man" or remember
those things that were once most precious to him,
beyond any thought of King or Country.

So what of the play's final scene? Is it or isn't it triumphal?

In traditional providentialist readings, the play's ending is triumphal because the play is about the restoration of "Order". The 10,000-strong English army with its grateful Scottish contingent meets with little resistance. As Old Siward, the English Lord of Northumberland, observes with relief and delight: "So great a day as this is cheaply bought." The "tyrant" is slain and beheaded by Macduff, Order is restored, and, once it is safe for him to do so, Malcolm enters the castle. Pointing to the "usurper's cursed head", Macduff declares that "The time is free" and hails Malcolm as the new King of Scotland, "for so thou art".

The play then ends with the speech in which the new King immediately uses the royal "We", dismisses the dead Macbeth and Lady Macbeth as "this dead butcher, and his fiend-like queen", and thanks God for providing "the grace of Grace" that has put him on the throne. Although he doesn't mention his countrymen's sufferings, he tells his loyal Scottish "thanes and kinsmen" that they all now have the English title of "earls, the first that Scotland/ In such an honour named"; he adds, sounding like his father, that they, as well as the English, can expect further rewards as soon as he can "reckon with your several loves,/ And make us even with you".

In the late 1950s, the providentialist view of *Macbeth* and its triumphal final scene was dominant. For critics like Irving Ribner – as for L.C. Knights years earlier and Sir Peter Hall in 1970 – the play's "dominant theme" was the "idea" that "through the working out of evil in a harmonious order good must emerge". Even a self-declared Marxist critic like Paul Siegel unhesitatingly aligned himself with Christian critics like Roy Battenhouse, Roy Walker and G.R. Elliott when he explained how "Nature violently expels Macbeth" for having "violated" its "laws".

There are, however, two major obstacles to supposing that the final scene is triumphal, and not yet another "seeming comfort" from which "discomfort" will suddenly "swell". The first is that the Weird Sisters' prophecy about Banquo begetting a line of kings has not come to pass: where, the German dramatist Bertolt Brecht wanted to know, was Fleance? Would he ever become King? And if so, how? The second is that we can only believe in a triumphal conclusion if we stifle our ominous sense that we have been here before – since the allegedly triumphal conclusion recalls so much that we saw in the early scenes.

The parallels are too many to discount. Macduff's longing to confront Macbeth "front to front" recalls the earlier "point to point" confrontation between Macbeth and the Thane of Cawdor. In the final scene Macbeth is decapitated and brandished on a pike; earlier, when he had been unseamed by Macbeth, Macdonwald's head was fixed upon the battlements. Duncan had to depend on Macbeth's prowess in butchering to secure his realm, just as Malcolm has to depend upon Macduff to kill Macbeth – and when Macduff does that he, like Macbeth, is killing a properly crowned and "anointed" King. Wilbur Sanders says that a "vague, free-floating sense that the old cycle is starting over again" is also evoked by "the deluge of *Hails* that greets Malcolm's reign, as the witches hailed Macbeth's". Equally, Macolm's "What's more to do/Which would be planted newly with the time" echoes Duncan's metaphor when he addresses Macbeth at their first (and only) onstage meeting: "I have begun to plant thee and will labor/ To make thee full of growing."

Then there is the fact that Macbeth has towered above all of the men who survive him in the final scene; he was not only more courageous but far more sensitive than the newly crowned Malcolm who so confidently and jarringly dismisses him as a "dead butcher". That in turn reminds us of his father's way of trying to impose moral order on the ghastly reports of "doubtful" conflicts where the outcome more obviously depended on Macbeth's prodigious courage and butcherly skills than on right or providence or what Malcolm vacuously calls "the grace of grace". L.C. Knights thinks that Malcolm's final speech provides

> a fitting close for a play in which moral law has been made present to us not as convention or command but as the law of life itself, as that which makes for life, and through which alone man can ground himself on, and therefore in some measure know, reality.

Critics, too, have made much of the symbolic felicitousness of the moving of Birnam Wood against Macbeth, as if Nature itself is rising against him. But it is not. Men are carrying the branches, and the battle depends on man-to-man combat: no sooner has Old Siward said "So great a day as this is cheaply bought" than he is shown his dead son. If we are to share Knights's happiness, we must stifle the feeling that the old cycle could easily begin again, and Malcolm's speech does nothing to dispel this feeling.

When Malcolm dismisses Macbeth and Lady Macbeth as "this dead Butcher, and his Fiend-like Queene", it should produce a tremor of protest – Macbeth was more than that, and fiends do not commit suicide – and also a tremor of premonitory alarm: the first Thane of Cawdor, after all, who was initially seen as a "Gentleman" became "that most disloyall Traytor", and Macbeth's butchery in killing him in Act One brought nothing but praise.

And yet while the providentalist critics of this play are not convincing, there *is* something very equivocal about the end, as about so much of the action. We *do* have a sense of something being "released" by Duncan's murder, just as there is *some* sense of closure, of a process working itself out, in the world of Day in which the action ends; the trouble is that such impressions of a natural order are constantly besieged by a battery of opposed impressions – of terrors that cannot be ordered or contained, and erupt from this play's world of Night.

As Stephen Booth puts it:

Finality is regularly unattainable throughout *Macbeth*. Macbeth and Lady Macbeth cannot get the murder of Duncan finished: Lady Macbeth has to go back with the knives. They cannot get done with Duncan himself: his blood will not wash off. Banquo refuses death in two ways: he comes back as a ghost, and (supposedly) he lives on in the line of Stuart kings into the actual present of the audience. The desirability and impossibility of conclusion is a regular concern of the characters, both in large matters ("The time has been/That, when the brains were out, the man would die,/ And there an end" (3.4)) and in such smaller ones as Macbeth's inability to achieve the temporary finality of sleep and Lady Macbeth's inability to

cease her activity even in sleep itself.

Many modern productions have cast doubt on the seemingly triumphal ending, and used different theatrical tactics to do so. In Trevor Nunn's 1976 production, the assembled thanes were not jubilant but very edgy. As Marvin Rosenberg put it in his *The Masks of Macbeth*: "The lights went down on a circle of drear men, eyeing each other and their new king without hope." Or, as Egil Törnqvist puts it in *Transposing Drama* (1991): "The final impression seems to be: health is restored – but for how long?" Four years later, in his production for the *BBC-Time Life* series, Jack Gold had his Fleance suddenly appear beside the dead Macbeth and stare at Malcolm, who was unnerved by this and unable to put on his crown. Other stagings have included a similarly scary reminder that Scotland's future may be less than radiant by letting the audience hear the Weird Sisters cackle, or by showing their presence in the final scene – and sometimes in many other scenes. Roman Polanski's 1971 film of *Macbeth* went further by adding a final scene that shows King Malcolm's brother Donalbain riding across the blasted heath to find the witches. As the American critic Pauline Kael commented, Polanski was making it clear that "the cycle of bloodletting is about to begin again".

Opposite: Orson Welles as Macbeth, 1948

Is life a tale "told by an idiot/Signifying nothing"?

This book has questioned the providentialist interpretations of *Macbeth* which for so long dominated not just critical accounts of the play but stage performances too. In a sense we have only been ready to think – or *really* think – about this play in the last 50 years or so.

In considering *Macbeth* it is worth briefly remembering how outdated the Romantic view of nature now seems. The skylark's song filled

CHRISTIAN IMAGERY IN
MACBETH

Macbeth's preoccupation with good and evil is vividly conveyed in its language and imagery. This is a play, says Victor Kiernan, about a man who "is anguished by knowing that he has bartered the gold of men's esteem for the tinsel of sovereignty". Marilyn French comments that after the murder of Duncan, instead of "procreation and felicity, the end of power becomes more power alone, consolidation and extension of power: thus, life becomes hell."

As these critics suggest, and as Arthur Kinney puts it in *Lies Like Truth*, the play is saturated with religious situations, ideas and images. To take just a few examples: Macbeth sees winds "fight/ Against the Churches" (4.1); he asks one of the murderers if he is morally prepared for Banquo's death: "Are you so Gospell'd to pray for this

Shelley's heart with joy, and made him think of the human soul. But in the last half century it affected poets like Ted Hughes very differently, so that in his poem "Skylarks" he ponders the nature of "Nature" and the bankrupted Romantic tradition of writing and dreaming about a "Nature" that was not (as Tennyson put it) red in tooth and claw:

> *I suppose you just gape and let your gaspings.*
> *Rip in and out through your voicebox*
> *O lark.*
> *And sing inwards as well as outwards.*

good man..?" (3.1); he calls the sacred majesty of Duncan "the Lords anointed Temple" (2.3); Banquo, meanwhile, would rest his life in the "great Hand of God" (2.3) and in her madness Lady Macbeth is one who "More needs the Divine, than the Physitian". (5.1) Even Macbeth's final despairing speech – "To morrow, and to morrow, and to morrow,/Creepes in this petty pace from day to day" (5.5) – draws on the dusty death of Psalm 22:15, the candle of Job 18:6, the walking shadow of Psalm 39:6 and the idiot's tale of Psalm 90:9.

Kinney describes *Macbeth* as a Doomsday play which draws heavily on biblical imagery – "that the play was about the end of the world is inescapable," he says. When Lady Macbeth commands her husband to wash his bloodied hands –

> *Goe get some Water,*
> *And wash this filthie Witnesse*
> *from your hand* [2.2]

– her words recall Christ's words to Pilate that his death should bear witness unto truth, and Macbeth's reply:

> *No, this my hand will rather*
> *The multitudinous Seas*
> *incarnadine,*

Like a breaker of ocean milling the shingle
                              O lark
O song, incomprehensibly both ways –
Joy! Help! Joy! Help!
                              O lark

Both the "O lark" refrain in this third section of a long poem and Hughes's earlier reminder that the lark is "Crueller than owl or eagle" suggest how his poem presents a representatively modern, anti-Romantic response to the ways that Shelley thinks

Making the Greene one, Red

echoes Revelation 16:3. When Lennox describes the night of Duncan's death

> *Where we lay,*
> *Our chimneys were blowne*
>   *down, and, as they say,*
> *Lamentings heard i' the air;*
>   *strange screams of death,*
> *And prophesying, with accents*
>   *terrible,*
> *Of dire combustion, and,*
>   *confused events,*
> *New hatch'd to the woeful time.*
>   *the obscure bird*
> *Clamor'd the livelong night.*
>   *some say, the earth*
> *Was feverous, and did shake*
>   *[2.3]*

he is citing eight of the traditional signs of the Last Judgement which were still pictured on church walls, in stained glass, and, during the childhood of playgoers in 1606, in the children's picture books of the Bible.

In the final act, Macduff calls for trumpets – "Make all our Trumpets speak, giue the all breath/Those clamorous Harbingers of Blood, & Death". (5.6) The trumpet, as in George Gascoigne's *Droomme of Doomes Day* (1576, 1586), is the trumpet announcing the Last Judgement.

"If, in the Christian sense, the only true tragedy is to forfeit one's soul," says about birds and the nature of Nature.

There is a similar contrast between the reactions of the Victorian poet and Jesuit Gerard Manley Hopkins and Hamlet when they look up at the night sky, as all of us do. In his early sonnet "The Starlight Night", Hopkins summons up a kind of rapt and religious ecstacy:

> *Look at the stars! look, look up at the skies!*
> *O look at all the fire-folk sitting in the air!*
> *The bright boroughs, the circle-citadels there...*

Edward Wagenknecht, "then Macbeth has a strong claim to be regarded as Shakespeare's Christian tragedy." As many critics have noted, the imagery of Macbeth is very patterned. "It lives more exclusively than any other Shakespearian tragedy on such simple, basic dualisms as day and night, summer and winter, brightness and murk," writes Michael Long. "It gives the impression of having been conceived whole, in a single instant..."

As Long also notes, the sacred imagery of Macbeth incorporates the pagan-sacred as well as the Christian-sacred.

Sacred images abound. We have the feast, the table and the cauldron; the sword and the dagger; the forest, the castle, the bed, the tomb; childbirth, murder and sacrifice; wounds and blood; armour and royal robes; old men with white beards and young men "in their first of manhood". It often seems to have less in common with other Shakespearian plays than it has with highly symbolic works, like the songs of Blake or *The Rime of the Ancient Mariner*, where we have rare, uncluttered access to the naked essentials of things.◆

On the other hand, Hamlet's response to the "canopy" or "majestic roof" of the sky at night and whatever lies beyond it is riven, rather than driven, as we might expect from the character who says or fears that "There is nothing either good or bad, but thinking makes it so":

I have of late – but wherefore I know not – lost all my mirth, foregone all custom of exercise; and indeed it goes so heavily with my disposition that this goodly frame, the earth, seems to me a sterile promontory. This most excellent canopy, the air, look you, this brave o'erhanging firmament, this majestic roof fretted with golden fire – why, it appears no other thing to me than a foul and pestilential congregation of vapours.

In this passage and elsewhere, Hamlet's intensely self-aware use of words like "appears" and "seems" shows that he recognises how his own state of mind may be turning the "majestic roof" (that he so richly describes) into a "sterile promontory". But, even when we have followed Hamlet by allowing for that, there is no Hopkinsian, religious dimension; rather, this universe remains mysterious – a great unknown. As Hamlet famously says: "There are more things in heaven and earth, Horatio,/ Than are dreamt of in your philosophy".

But Hamlet does not presume to know

whatever these "things" are, and the world of *Macbeth* is much closer to his world, and to the world of Ted Hughes, than it is to the world of Gerard Manley Hopkins or Shelley – or Wordsworth, who became Shakespeare's historical rival as the "poet of Nature". When A.P. Rossiter compared these two "poets of Nature" in the last, inevitably contoversial or combustible chapter of *Angel with Horns* (1961), his main objection to "the national park of Wordsworthian Nature" is that Wordsworth's "vision" of Nature was "so highly selective and exclusive", whereas Shakespeare is far more aware – above all in *King Lear* and *Macbeth* – of what Rossiter memorably calls "under-nature".

Wilbur Sanders was surely right to protest, in 1963, that there is "a primacy of evil in the world" of *Macbeth*. The feeling is, he says, that the "capacity for destruction defeats that of goodness for reconstruction. Its assault is not upon the mediocre but upon the best. And its presence in the world of the play is somehow too intense, too real, too pressing to permit us finally to subsume it under goodness, or providence, or nature."

Banquo's wry comment that "There's Husbandry in Heaven" – not unlike Woody Allen's description of God as an "under-achiever" – catches the mood of this play, which never denies the existence of "Order" in some dogmatically sceptical or nihilistic way but makes reality seem alarmingly uncertain. The critic Arthur Sewell astutely points out that all the central images of the play – blood, sleep, night – "evoke in us the very act of annihilating real and solid things, of making blurred the outlines of objects, of mantling the surfaces with darkness".

So what role does Christianity play in the world of *Macbeth*? We have noted that Macbeth himself takes a Christian view of the world, and that it is this which makes his transformation into a monster so terrifying. The world of *Macbeth* is a world of Christian beliefs even if it is not, in a broader sense, a Christian world. This is a play, says Sanders in an eloquent passage,

> fed at its sources by the ethics of Jesus. For the creating mind that fuses imaginative identification *with* Macbeth, and a moral judgement *on* Macbeth, into a single act of dramatic recognition, is one which has grown accustomed to stretching itself Christianly between trenchant judgement and wise suspension of judgement. Its poise and assurance is supported by the Christianity it has breathed from its earliest years. Which does not necessarily mean that Shakespeare was a 'believer' in the conventional sense – George Eliot in *Middlemarch* seems to have drawn a similar strength from a Christianity she rejected – but that he was supported in a thousand indefinable ways by the Christian climate in which he lived. He

could take these things for granted, did not need to be noisily assertive about them, could rest in them.

It is with this in mind that we must approach Macbeth's final despairing soliloquies in Act Five:

To-morrow, and to-morrow, and to-morrow
Creeps in this petty pace from day to day
To the last syllable of recorded time,
And all our yesterdays have lighted fools
The way to dusty death. Out, out, brief candle!
Life's but a walking shadow, a poor player
That struts and frets his hour upon the stage
And then is heard no more. It is a tale
Told by an idiot, full of found and fury,
Signifying nothing. [5.5]

They are bitter, disappointed words, the words of a man driven mad by his actions, a man who has killed the better part of himself and is watching his soul die. But how much do they reflect the world of the play? Could Macbeth in his disillusion, be right?

The play, as we have seen, is much more equivocal than most critics allow. Its characters, including Macbeth, appear to be the products and victims of an unaccommodating if not hostile universe – a universe which raises questions not just about the existence of free will but also about the whole notion of good and evil, external order or permanent values. "There are no moral facts whatsoever," says Nietzsche in *The Twilight of the Idols*; to Wittgenstein, in *Philosophical Investigations*, values can never be "read off" as part of the world's fabric and furniture; J.M. Mackie's admirably incisive book *Ethics* begins: "There are no objective values." These philosophers, surely, come closer to explaining the view of life we find in *Macbeth* than the comforting views of many traditional critics.

And, as we have seen, modern critics like Sanders, in their Nietzschean readings of the play, see in Macbeth a defiant energy which raises him above simple butchery and makes judging him much more difficult. The play conveys a sense of the danger and potential destructiveness of all human action, especially action motivated by ambition. There is something, says Michael Long,

> fatal, doomed, but heroic about Macbeth, and something which makes him not the disruptive outsider of whom the world is well rid but the representative outsider, the outsider such as we all are, the archetypal representative of the fact that, as conscious, acting individuals, not trees in the forest, we cannot simply stand 'in the hand of the great God' but are fated to be involved in deeds.

In this respect, says Long, *Macbeth* echoes the Christian myth of the Fall. Milton once considered tackling Macbeth as a dramatic subject and in a sense, as Long says, he did tackle it in *Paradise Lost*. For Milton's Satan shares with Macbeth the "paradoxical mixture of criminality and greatness". And there are frequent "pessimistic intuitions" in *Macbeth* of "the criminal but heroic nature of all human doing or agency".

There are also, as Long says, echoes of *Macbeth* in Wagner's *The Ring*: the sunlit world of rivers and forests is akin to Macbeth's "innocent world of the martlets, the 'delicate' air and the green boughs of Birnam Wood. The darkness into which it declines is akin to the murk and perversion of Macbeth's 'fog and filthy air'." In both works, "the primal crime is the interventionist deed of a great and reckless creature" and in Macbeth there is "something of a Wagnerian sense of an irremediable tragedy in the very fabric of things caused by the fact that deeds are endemic to the business of being alive and conscious and yet at the same time are ruinous in their effects".

It is worth noting, finally, that the world of *Macbeth* is a very lonely world. It is full of "lonely talking", in Michael Long's phrase; nowhere else in Shakespeare's works is there quite so much continuous self-communing, self-interrogation and confession as there is in *Macbeth*, and one of the impressions this gives, "as part of the bedrock of the play's vision", is of "a primitive, largely nocturnal loneliness in creatural life, conveyed by the cries both of animals and of men and witnessed to by all sorts of lonely talking". Ultimately, in an unaccommodating universe, *Macbeth* suggests, man is alone. The bonds he forms with others are as fragile as the values by which he lives in a world he can never fully understand.

In Shakespeare's lifetime the new astronomy of Copernicus and Galileo had decentred man, Machiavelli's revolutionary political theories had challenged traditional notions of degree, and Montaigne's sceptical essays had undermined traditional ideas about the self and natural law. As John Donne reflected in his poem *The First Anniversary*:

> And new Philosophy calls all in doubt:
> 'Tis all in pieces, all coherence gone;
> All just supply, and all Relation.

In the last half century scientific advances, notably in physics, biology and the cognitive sciences, have brought a comparable upheaval and sense of crisis. As James Watson Cronin, who won the 1980 Nobel prize for physics, observed in a 2007 conference on astro-particle physics: "We think we understand the universe, but we only understand four per cent of everything."

According to the most recent models, 73 percent of cosmic energy seems to consist of "dark energy" and 23 per cent of "dark matter," the pervasive but unidentified stuff that holds the universe together and accelerates its expansion. The remaining four per cent consists of so-called "normal matter" such as atoms and molecules.

As Stephen Booth has observed, "*Macbeth* puts us through an actual experience of the insufficiency of our finite minds to the infinite universe." Earlier critics didn't think that, but it should now be easier for us to be – or more difficult not to be – alive to the terrors of *Macbeth*, and the uncertainties it provokes about the nature of "Nature".

Sean Bean and Samantha Bond at the Albery Theatre, 2002

A SHORT CHRONOLOGY

1040 Macbeth kills Duncan

1057 Macbeth killed

1527 Hector Boece publishes his *Scotorum Historiae*, a history of the Scottish people, which argues that the Stewart kings were descended from Banquo. In fact, Banquo is Boece's own invention.

1564 Shakespeare born in Stratford-upon-Avon

1587 Holinshed's *Chronicles*, a history of England, Scotland and Ireland familiar to Shakespeare and his contemporaries.

1603 Queen Elizabeth 1 dies; accession of King James 1. It has been suggested that the relative brevity of Macbeth was an indication of the new king's notoriously short attention span, but, as Peter Ackroyd says in his biography of Shakespeare, this seems unlikely.

1603 A parliamentary act to "restrain the abuse of players" forbids irreverence or blasphemy on the public stage, which may explain the notable lack of oaths and profanities in *Macbeth*.

1605 Discovery of Guy Fawkes's plot to blow up the Houses of Parliament. King James I greeted by three sibyls at the gates of an Oxford College and hailed as the true descendant of Banquo.

1606 It is hard to date *Macbeth* precisely. This is probably the year it was written, though it might have been earlier.

1616 Shakespeare dies on the 23rd April.

1623 *Macbeth* printed as part of the First Folio.

1667 Samuel Pepys describes Sir William Davenant's "operatic" version of Macbeth as "one of the best plays for a stage... that I ever saw". Many subsequent productions were based on Davenant's adaptation of the text.

1823 Thomas de Quincey's famous essay, 'On the Knocking at the Gate in *Macbeth*'.

1904 A.C. Bradley's hugely influential Shakespearian Tragedy.

1933 L.C. Knights publishes 'How Many Children Had Lady Macbeth?'

1963 Wilbur Smith's essay, 'The Strong Pessimism of Macbeth'.

1957 A famous Japanese film version of *Macbeth*, *Throne of Blood*, later described by Professor Harold Bloom as "the most successful film version of *Macbeth*".

1976 Trevor Nunn's Royal Shakespeare Company production of *Macbeth*, with Ian McKellen and Judi Dench. One of the best-received 20th-century productions, later filmed for television.

BIBLIOGRAPHY

Aitchison, Ian, *Macbeth: Man and Myth*, Sutton, 1999

Auden, W.H., *Lectures on Shakespeare*, Princeton, 2000

Auerbach, Erich, *Mimesis: The Representation of Reality in Western Literature* (originally published in Germany in 1946), Princeton, 2003

Berger, Harry, Jr, *Making Trifles of Terrors,* Stanford University Press, 1997

Bevington, David, *Tudor Drama and Politics*, Harvard 1968

Booth, Stephen, K*ing Lear, Macbeth, Indefinition, and Tragedy,* Yale, 1983

Bradley, A.C., *Shakespearean Tragedy*, Macmillan, 1904

Brooks, Cleanth, "The Naked Babe and the Cloak of Maniless" in *The Well Wrought Urn: Studies in the Structure of Poetry,* San Diego: Harcourt, 1974

Coleridge, Samuel Taylor, *Lectures and Notes on Shakspere and Other English Poets*, London: George Bell and Sons, 1904

Danby, John, *Shakespeare's Doctrine of Nature*, Faber and Faber, 1949

De Quincey, Thomas, "On the Knocking at the Gate in Macbeth", first published in the *London Magazine*, October 1823

Granville-Barker, Harley, *Prefaces to Shakespeare*, 1946, Princeton University Press

Janouch, Gustav, *Conversations with Kafka*, New Directions, 1971

Kinney, Arthur F., *Lies Like Truth*, Wayne State University Press, 2001

Knights, L.C. Explorations, *Essays in Criticism mainly on the Literature of the Seventeenth Century*, Chatto & Windus, 1946

Long, Michael, *Macbeth: Harvester New Critical Introductions to Shakespeare*, Harvester Wheatsheaf, 1989

Muir, Kenneth and Schoenbaum, S., eds., *A New Companion to Shakespeare Studies*, Cambridge University Press, 1971

Nuttall, A.D., *Shakespeare The Thinker*, Yale, 2007

Rosenberg, Marvin, *Masks of Macbeth*, University of Delaware Press, 1993

Sanders, Wilbur, *The Dramatist and the Received Idea*, Cambridge University Press, 1968

Törnqvist, Egil, T*ransposing Drama*, Macmillan, 1991

Tredell, Nicolas, ed., *Shakespeare: Macbeth: a reader's guide to essential criticism*, Palgrave Macmillan, 2006

Wain, John, ed., *Shakespeare: Macbeth: a selection of critical essays* (Casebook series), Macmillan, 1968

Wilson Knight, G., *The Wheel of Fire*, Routledge, 1930

INDEX

First published in 2012 by
Connell Guides
Spye Arch House
Spye Park
Lacock
Chippenham
Wiltshire SN15 2PR

10 9 8 7 6 5 4 3 2 1

Picture credits:
p.17 © Moviestore Collection Ltd/Alamy
p.66 © Alamy
p.67 © Corbis
p.74 © Alamy
p.95 @ National Portrait Gallery
p.106 © Corbis
p.119 © Lebrecht

A CIP catalogue record for this book is available from the British Library.
ISBN 978-1-907776-04-5

Editorial assistant: Katie Sanderson
Typesetting: Katrina ffiske
Design © Nathan Burton
Printed in Great Britain by Butler Tanner and Dennis

www.connellguides.com